HOLISTIC LEARNING:

A Teacher's Guide to Integrated Studies

John P. Miller

J. R. Bruce Cassie

Susan M. Drake

Curriculum Series 59

OISE Press

The Ontario Institute for Studies in Education

A Project Sponsored by the Superintendents' Curriculum Cooperative

The Ontario Institute for Studies in Education has three prime functions: to conduct programs of graduate study in education, to undertake research in education, and to assist in the implementation of the findings of educational studies. The Institute is a college charted by an Act of the Ontario Legislature in 1965. It is affiliated with the University of Toronto for graduate studies purposes.

The publications program of the Institute has been established to make available information and materials arising from studies in education, to foster the spirit of critical inquiry, and to provide a forum for the exchange of ideas about education. The opinions expressed should be viewed as those of the contributors.

© The Ontario Institute for Studies in Education 1990
252 Bloor Street West
Toronto, Ontario
M5S 1V6

Editor: Anne Webb
Layout Artists: Sharon Richmond and Sheila Barnard
Printer: Alger Press Ltd.

Canadian Cataloguing in Publication Data

Miller, John P., 1943-
Holistic learning : a teacher's guide to
integrated studies

(Curriculum series ; 59)
"A project sponsored by the Superintendents'
Curriculum Cooperative."
Includes bibliographical references.
ISBN 0-7744-0358-6

1. Interdisciplinary approach in education.
2. Teaching - Philosophy. 3. Mythology - Study
and teaching. I. Cassie, J. R. Bruce (James Robert
Bruce). II. Drake, Susan M., 1944-
III. Ontario Institute for Studies in Education.
IV. Title. V. Series: Curriculum series (Ontario
Institute for Studies in Education) ; 59.

LB1025.2.M55 1990   370'.1   C90-095501-5

ISBN 0-7744-0358-6   Printed in Canada
    2 3 4 5   AP   49 39 29 19

TABLE OF CONTENTS

CHAPTER 4   DEVELOPING UNITS IN INTEGRATED STUDIES / 102

CHAPTER 5   IMPLEMENTING INTEGRATED STUDIES / 115

ACKNOWLEDGMENTS

This guide has been prepared with the financial support of the Superintendents' Curriculum Cooperative. We would like to thank the superintendents for their encouragement, feedback, and support.

Also, we would like to thank the many individuals who gave us helpful comments on the first draft of the book. Along with responses from several Ontario school board personnel, our work was reviewed by Florence Maynes, Floyd Robinson, John Ross, and Dennis Thiessen. Although we have not incorporated all suggestions, we feel that our reviewers have made a significant contribution to the quality of this final draft.

We want to express our appreciation for the (thoughtful) editing which Anne Webb has done on this book.

Finally, we would like to thank Joan Graziani for typing the manuscript with such care.

John P. Miller
J.R. Bruce Cassie
Susan M. Drake

CHAPTER 1

INTRODUCTION

This book outlines strategies to facilitate holistic learning, that is, learning that makes connections. For example, there can be connections between subjects or between thinking and intuition. The particular focus of this guide is on subject connections — on facilitating holistic learning through integrated studies in the intermediate division. Before we introduce strategies for facilitating holistic learning, we will outline a rationale for integrated studies and present a framework for approaching subject integration.

RATIONALE FOR INTEGRATED STUDIES

One of the main problems facing both educators and Western society in general is fragmentation. The results of this fragmentation of life have taken such forms as acid rain and other pollutions which have occurred because we have separated our economic activity from the environment in which this activity takes place. In schools fragmentation reveals itself, particularly at the intermediate and secondary levels, when we focus on individual subjects without attempting to show the interconnections among subjects. The problem, then, is that students often are confronted with long lists of facts or skills that are isolated both from each other and, more importantly, from a pattern or context that would connect and give meaning to the information. Integrated studies is a vehicle for addressing the problem of fragmentation.

In our daily lives we tend to approach problems, or life situations, holistcally rather than from the standpoint of a single discipline. In deciding who to vote for we do not rely on a course we may have taken in political science; instead, we pull together our accumulated wisdom and knowledge to make our decision. In short, the "real world" demands an integrated response. The demand for integration does not mean that individual subjects are not viable organizers of learning — we need some way of presenting concepts and skills to students systematically. However, often students cannot connect what they have learned in one particular subject or discipline to other subjects. Again, integrated studies attempts to facilitate the transfer of knowledge and skills across disciplines.

An integrated approach is also consistent with the Ministry of Education's stated education goals and their image of the learner. This image focuses on the student as a "self-motivated, self-directed problem-solver ... who is capable of inquiry, analysis, synthesis and evaluation," and who is also a "perceptive discoverer capable of resourcefulness, intuition and creativity" (Ontario Ministry of Education, 1988, p. 6). Such an image encourages integrated studies since the focus is not on recalling information, but on analytic and creative thinking that tends to span various disciplines.

Integrated studies also offers a way of dealing with the problem of curriculum overload. Teachers at all levels complain about how they are required to "add on" new initiatives to their current programs. Integration is a way of bringing much of the curriculum together so that the teacher is able to deal with several topics, skills, and concepts at once rather than as separate subjects. In sum, an integrated studies program deserves serious consideration because it can begin to deal with the problems of fragmentation, transfer of learning, and curriculum overload, and is congruent with the Ministry's image of the learner.

HOLISTIC CURRICULUM: A FRAMEWORK FOR INTEGRATED LEARNING

Integrated studies implies a holistic approach to learning and to curriculum since both the terms "integrated" and "holistic" imply the notion of connectedness. Below is a definition of holistic curriculum which captures this notion:

> The focus of holistic education is on relationships — the relationship between linear thinking and intuition, the relationship between mind and body, the relationships between various domains of knowledge, the relationship between the individual and community and the relationship between self and Self. In the holistic curriculum the student examines these relationships so that he/she gains both an awareness of them and the skills necessary to transform the relationships where it is appropriate. (Miller, 1988, p. 3)

The connections this definition centers on can be explored in a number of different contexts. Five of those contexts are briefly outlined below:

Linear Thinking and Intuition. The holistic curriculum attempts to restore a balance between linear thinking and intuition. Various techniques such as metaphor and visualization can be integrated with more traditional thinking approaches so that a synthesis is achieved.

Relationship Between Mind and Body. The holistic curriculum explores the relationship between mind and body so that the student senses the connection between the two. The relationship can be explored by movement, dance, and relaxation or "centering" exercises.

Relationships Among Domains of Knowledge. There are many different ways we can connect academic disciplines and school subjects. The way in which interdisciplinary approaches to thinking can show how subjects are related is more fully developed in the remainder of this book.

Relationship Between self and Community. The holistic curriculum sees the student in relation to community. Community refers to the school community, the community of one's town and nation, and the global community. The student develops interpersonal skills, community service skills, and social action skills.

Relationship Between self and Self. Ultimately, the holistic curriculum lets us connect with the deepest part of ourselves. Ralph Waldo Emerson said:

> A man(sic) finds out there is somewhat in him that knows more than he does. Then he comes presently to the curious question, Who's who? which of these two is really me? the one that knows more or the one that knows less: the little fellow or the big fellow? (Emerson, 1909-14, Vol. 9, p. 190)

How do we connect with the big fellow or the Self? One way is through the arts. The music of Mozart, Handel, Schubert, and Bach are excellent vehicles for developing this deeper connection. Another means is through mythologies which deal with the universal concerns of human beings. The application of mythologies is discussed in Chapter 2 of this guide as a strategy for personal growth and subject integration.

Another way of clarifying what is meant by holistic education is to compare this approach to other approaches to education. Identifying three basic positions on the function of schooling is helpful in analyzing and describing the range of views held on curriculum and instruction (Miller, 1983, 1986, 1987; Miller & Seller, 1985). Each position is rooted in a world view that can be linked to various philosophical, psychological, and social contexts. Following are brief descriptions of the three positions — transmission, transaction, and transformation.

The *transmission position* holds that the function of curriculum is to transmit facts, skills, and values to students. The student tends to be considered a passive receptor of knowledge. The transmission position stresses mastery of traditional school subjects through traditional teaching methods, particularly textbook learning. The students acquire basic skills, and cultural values and mores that are necessary to function in society. The position also stresses the application to curriculum planning of a mechanistic view of human behaviour, whereby student skills are developed through specific instructional strategies. The movement involved in conveying skills, knowledge, and values to students is one-way (see Figure 1.1). The philosophical-scientific paradigm for this position is an atomistic view of the universe in which reality is seen to consist of separate, isolated building blocks.

TRANSMISSION POSITION

Figure 1.1

The *transaction position* identifies the individual as rational and capable of intelligent problem solving. Education is viewed as a dialogue between the student and the curriculum (see Figure 1.2); it is a process in which the student reconstructs knowledge through dialogue. The central elements in the transaction position are: curriculum strategies that facilitate problem solving; the application of problem solving to general social contexts and within the framework of a democratic process; and development of cognitive skills within the academic disciplines. The philosophical-scientific paradigm for the transaction position is the scientific method which has dominated the Western world since the Enlightenment.

TRANSACTION POSITION

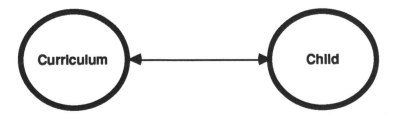

Figure 1.2

The *transformation position* focuses on personal and social change. The student is actively involved in all phases of the learning process. The position encompasses three specific orientations: skills that promote personal and social transformation; a vision of social change that leads to harmony with the environment rather than control over the environment; and the attribution of a spiritual dimension to the environment. The paradigm for the transformation position is based on an ecologically interdependent conception of nature that emphasizes the interrelatedness of phenomena. As shown in Figure 1.3 below, the curriculum and the student interpenetrate each other in a holistic manner.

TRANSFORMATION POSITION

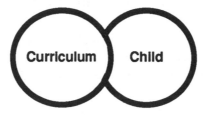

Figure 1.3

What is the relationship between the three positions? They can be seen as competing alternatives where choosing one position excludes the others; or, alternatively, each position can be seen as more inclusive than the one prior to it. From this latter framework, the transaction position includes the transmission position focus on knowledge retention and applies it to problem solving. In turn, the transformation position with its holistic emphasis incorporates the cognitive emphasis of the transaction position within a broader, more inclusive context. It is possible, then, to view the three positions as intersecting circles (see Figure 1.4).

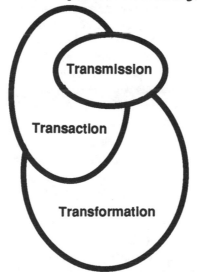

Figure 1.4

Note. Figures from *The Holistic Curriculum* (pp. 4-7) by J. P. Miller, 1988, Toronto: OISE Press. Copyright 1988 by OISE Press.

In holistic education we attempt to facilitate a broadening of visions and perspectives. We move from the more restrictive scope of an atomistic perspective to a more inclusive view that witnesses the connections between ourselves and many levels of experience and knowledge.

INTEGRATED STUDIES AND THE HOLISTIC CURRICULUM

Holistic curriculum provides a framework for approaching integrated studies. At a transmission level, studies are integrated by linking the *content* of different subjects. Thus, in studying Ancient Greece, art and literature are included in a study of the historical period. At the transactional level, integrated studies is facilitated through *problem solving* and inquiry-based approaches. In studying Greece, a problem is presented to the students which allows them to connect various subjects and disciplines. Problem-solving models and thinking-skills approaches are helpful here in providing step-by-step learning sequences to facilitate the inquiry process. Problems can also be presented at the transformational level which incorporate intuition into the problem-solving process. At the transformational level, the teacher looks for *integrative patterns* that allow the student to place the information in a larger context. For example, the idea of symmetry can be used to connect art, math, and physics.

Dennis Thiessen (1989) has suggested the following relationship between the three positions and the integration of disciplines. The transmission position is viewed as *multidisciplinary* as a particular area or topic is investigated through different subjects; however, there is no attempt to link or integrate the subjects. The transaction position can be seen as *interdisciplinary* where questions or problems are explored through different processes and perspectives. At the transformation level integration is *transdisciplinary*, or nondisciplinary, where experiences are explored for their personal, social and educational meaning. At this level the student connects with herself or himself at a personal level, and with other people at a social level. The student also investigates issues or problems but is not bound by a particular discipline.

APPROACHES TO INTEGRATED STUDIES

This guide outlines strategies and ideas which correspond with, and are thereby legitimated by, the Ministry of Education's image of the learner and its thirteen goals of education which stress a transactional/transformational approach to curriculum. Since the holistic curriculum is an underlying frame for this guide, it should be noted that we tend to emphasize transformational approaches to integration. Given this framework and the Ministry's image of the learner, we do not cover all approaches to integration, particularly those of a multidisciplinary or transmission variety. Our approach to exploring integration is through two main areas: Human Themes and Human Processes (Thiessen, 1989).

Human Themes

Human themes focus on areas of human concern such as language, spirituality, and culture. We have focused on myth as an integration vehicle that also connects students to fundamental human themes. Mythology provides a broad set of connecting patterns that can link literature, history, art, and religion in a way that is personally meaningful to students. Joseph Campbell defines mythology as "a system of images that incorporates a concept of the universe as divinely energized and energizing ambience with which we live" (1981, p. 1). Campbell also comments on the need for a new global mythology that can provide transcendent meaning to our lives, and the former Ontario Deputy Ministry of Education, Bernard Shapiro (1988), stated: "A genuine sustaining myth must have some ultimate transcendent purpose, some sense of the good, and it is in its expression that we shall find a source for the mission of our common schools and our common destiny." Mythologies arise from the human being's deepest need to make sense of her or his role in the universe. The use of mythology, legends, and fairy tales has recently been stressed by the Ministry of Education in the resource document, *Growing with Book* (1988). We approach mythology in Chapter 2 with respect to how it can facilitate adolescents' struggles with questions that are unique to the intermediate-level stage of development.

Broad themes can also be used to facilitate subject integration. Paul Park (1983) describes how themes can be used in environmental studies to integrate subject matter. This example is transactional because the focus is on topic-based inquiry rather than on the development of personal meaning. Themes that are suggested for the junior level by Park include such seemingly disparate concepts as pioneers and paper towels. To start the unit on pioneers, Park recommends the technique of webbing or clustering which is often used in a thematic approach. Webbing starts with the central theme and then builds a set of sub-topics, issues, and questions around this theme. Figure 1.5 is the example of a web for pioneers.

Park describes how one teacher in London, Ontario, started the unit with a visit to a conservation area. The trip helped students to develop an interest in the lives of the early residents of southwestern Ontario. Students were interested in the kinds of clothes the people wore, the food they ate, and the homes they lived in. Student activities included constructing model villages, creating dolls and costumes, and making candles. Language arts activities involved writing poems and stories related to pioneer life.

Park also suggests guidelines for developing units in thematic studies. First, the teacher should identify two or three specific objectives and draw from at least two different disciplines. Second, the teacher and students should focus on a theme where they have both some interest and background. From this background the teacher should develop a clear set of expected student learning outcomes. Similarly, the teacher should be clear about the questions that will be pursued by the students. Park found that "if the children and teacher are not absolutely clear as to the question or issue under study, the end result will produce confused children, mediocre material and frustrated teachers" (p. 90). A third point made by Park is that students need training in data gathering skills. For example, students going through textual material should be able to summarize key

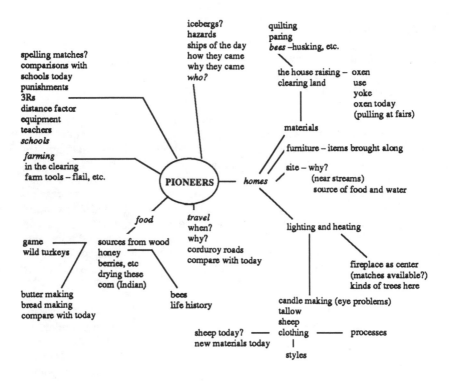

Figure 1.5

Note. From *A Canadian Social Studies* (p. 95) edited by J. Parsons, G. Milburn, and M. van Mansen, 1983, Edmonton, AB: University of Alberta. Copyright 1983 by University of Alberta. Reprinted by permission.

points and use cross-referencing and indexing. Interview skills also need to be worked on if interviews are part of the data gathering process. Finally, students need models and assistance with managing and organizing the data.

Human Processes

Human processes involve activities that allow humans to make sense and meaning out of life. According to Thiessen (1989), human processes include such things as a "sense of wonder (curiosity), an urge to discover, a need to unravel puzzles, issues or uncertainties, etc." In this guide we have focused on *problem solving* as a strategy which can facilitate the process of making sense and meaning. Since problem solving is central to the Ministry's image of the learner, and can also link various disciplines, we feel that it is a useful integrative strategy. The interdisciplinary skills list outlined in the Ontario Ministry of Education's History (1986) and Geography (1988) guidelines is an example of a strategy that can be applied to two different disciplines. These same skills have also been used in literature appreciation (Maynes & Ross, 1985). In Chapter 3, both transactional and transformational approaches to problem solving are discussed as potential vehicles for subject integration.

Another way of making sense in a transactional and transformational way is through the use of *metaphor*. Aristotle said that "the greatest thing by far is to be metaphorical ... that to metaphorize well is a sign of genius because [this ability] implies intuitive perception of the similarity inherent in the dissimilar" (cited in Sanders & Sanders, 1983, p. 127). Since using metaphors involves making connections between dissimilar concepts, this figure of speech is useful in a holistic approach to curriculum and, more specifically, in subject integration.

Williams (1983) has suggested a number of ways that metaphor can facilitate integrated learning. For example, the following question can facilitate connections between history and science: "How was the period leading up to the French Revolution like the building up of a thunderstorm?" (p. 71). The focus in this question is the French Revolution and the thunderstorm is used as a metaphor to facilitate an understanding of the causes of the revolution.

Bob Samples (1976) has described four levels of metaphoric teaching. The first level, the *symbolic*, is the most basic and involves substituting a verbal or visual symbol for an object or process. For example, the word horse may be used to symbolize the animal.

The next level, the *synergistic/comparative mode*, uses a comparison (e.g., road map and the circulatory system) so that the individual's understanding of the two factors is enhanced through the comparison. Parables and fables often use the synergistic mode to make a point.

Samples' third level is the *integrative mode*,whereby the individual integrates the metaphor and the material through the use of techniques such as visualization and role playing. For example, a guided imagery experience of the water cycle, where students visualize the cycle in their mind's eye, can facilitate the integrative mode in which the student engages the metaphor at a deeper, more personal level.

The final level is the *inventive*, through which the metaphor leads the individual to a new level of awareness and creative perception. Samples (1976) quotes Jonas Salk on this mode:

> The artist draws upon that part of the mind that functions beneath consciousness...while the scientist, by and large, but not exclusively, uses that part of the mind that functions in consciousness. The part of the mind that functions beneath consciousness also operates during consciousness.... It is necessary to learn how to draw more upon it and employ it for solving the problems of life, of survival and of evolution. Wisdom arises from both parts of the mind. (p. 100)

This level of metaphor is the level at which the person has the "aha" experience of seeing something for the first time.

Sanders and Sanders (1983) have also developed an approach to teaching creativity through metaphor that facilitates integration. There are four basic levels to their strategy which roughly parallel Samples' four levels of metaphoric teaching. At the first level, the *focus* level, the teacher identifies a metaphor to help students understand a concept. For example, the butterfly can be used as a metaphor for change and growth.

At the *personal comparison* level, the second level, the student compares herself or himself with the metaphor and thus develops a personal connection with the metaphor.

Next, at the *metaphoric interaction* level, the student begins to interact with the metaphor through use. This process often can involve discussion or use of guided imagery.

At the forth level, identified as *insight moments for concept mastery*, the teacher really begins to stretch the student by using improbable analogies to make the concept/metaphor connections.

Sanders and Sanders give several examples of how this process works in practice. One example is a unit on time which they argue is relevant to subjects such as science, mathematics, social studies, and language. For example, the beginning and development of the universe is studied in science, while infinity is a central concept in mathematics. Time is also a central concept in history as chronology is often a main organizer in the history curriculum. Language and dialects also change with time. The following explicates how the example of a unit on time can be conveyed through the four levels of metaphoric teaching.

Level 1: Focus Level

At this level the teacher can begin by presenting several images of time (e.g., clocks, watches, sundials, hourglasses and pictures of the seasons) to the students and then asking what these images have in common. Next, the teacher writes "TIME" on the board and asks the students what time means to them personally.

After this introduction to time, the teacher can present an initial idea or set of ideas that links the concept, metaphor, and subject. For example, if the students are studying monarchies in Europe, the teacher can read Percy Bysshe Shelley's poem, "Ozymandias":

> I met a traveller from an antique land
> Who said: "Two vast and trunkless legs of stone
> Stand in the desert. Near them, on the sand,
> Half sunk, a shattered visage lies, whose frown,
> And wrinkled lip, and sneer of cold command,
> Tell that its sculptor well those passions read
> Which yet survive, stamped on these lifeless things,
> The hand that mocked them and the heart that fed.
> And on the pedestal these words appear—

"My name is Ozymandias, king of kings:
Look on my works, ye Mighty, and despair!
Nothing beside remains. Round the decay
Of that colossal wreck, boundless and bare
The lone and level sands stretch far away."
(Cited in Williams, 1963, pp. 166-167.)

After reading the poem, the teacher can ask how the image of time described in the poem compares with time measured by clocks.

Students can begin to develop definitions of time. Sanders and Sanders have found that student generated definitions contain certain elements such as: a) time is part of a continuum of events; b) time is non-spatial in that it is not seen as something physically separate; c) time is irreversible; and d) time is a measured interval in an ongoing set of events. Student definitions can be compared to dictionary definitions.

This first level is primarily transactional in nature because the focus is conceptual. The next three levels are more transformation oriented because personal and imaginative connections are developed.

Level 2: The Personal Comparison
At this level, the teacher asks the student to consider how she or he is similar to the concept of time. For example, the teacher might ask: "How is the burning candle (the four seasons, the calendar, the stop watch, the metronome) like you?" (Sanders & Sanders, 1983, p. 77). The students can then share their responses once the teacher has developed a nonthreatening atmosphere for this activity. The Sanders have found that this activity tends to generate enthusiastic and imaginative discussion.

Level 3: The Metaphoric Interaction
Here the student interacts with the concept at the experiential level. For example, the students might visit a museum, see slides, or experience a guided fantasy journey. The Sanders present a guided imagery journey of the history of the earth. The journey is based on the research of James Rettie, which shows the history of the earth from its formation over the last 757 million years. Students then visualize all the stages of the earth's formation, the beginning of life, and the history of human life. Students are usually amazed by the length of time it took for the earth to cool down, the period of time that the dinosaurs lived on the earth, and the comparatively short period of time that humans have occupied the planet. The guided fantasy, debriefing questions, and possible student responses are included in the Sanders' text.

Level 4: Insight Moments for Concept Mastery
At this last level, the teacher presents the students with questions which are meant

to stimulate new insights into both the concept and metaphor. For the unit on time, the Sanders (1983) suggest breaking the students into small groups and then letting them discuss the following questions:

1. Time is a staircase for all our successes. Why?

2. If dinosaurs are grandfather clocks and ancient cities are sundials, what clock symbolizes our present [North] American society? Our classroom? Why?

3. How do trees tell time? Rivers tell time? Rocks tell time? Birds tell time?

4. Death is a sundial for every generation. Why?

5. Cancer is the twentieth century's stopwatch. Why?

6. History is a self-winding wristwatch. Explain.

7. Society is an alarm clock we need to wake us up. Why?

8. A novel is an hourglass that is ready to be turned over and over. Explain.

9. Science is a process that "tells time" by exploring nature. Show this to be true.

10. Math is having a clock that tells the correct time for any place on earth. (p. 86)

Notice how the questions cut across a number of disciplines. Sanders and Sanders comment: "You will find that any subject area can be enhanced by exploring its relationship to time factors and time concepts; crucial however, will be the illuminary moment when the metaphor and the subject content merge, expand understanding and become internalized" (p. 86).

SUMMARY

In this chapter, a case was made for holistic learning and integrated studies based on the Ministry's image of the learner and the problems of fragmentation and curriculum overload. We also presented the holistic curriculum as a framework for integrated studies. Finally, we outlined two broad areas for integration: human themes and human processes. Two brief examples of each were presented and in the next two chapters we develop in more detail the two strategies introduced: mythology and problem solving.

We would like to note here that we support David Hunt's (1987) notion of "Inside-Out" change. In other words, the strategies presented in this book must connect at some level to the inner life of the teacher; otherwise they will end up as transmission strategies devoid of personal meaning. Thus, we encourage teachers to reflect on the concepts and strategies presented in the following chapters in relation to their own experience. Teachers should feel free to adapt and modify the material so that it fits their own classroom. According to Schön (1983), practitioners are most effective when they can modify their technique, moment-to-moment, based on their own intuition.

REFERENCES

Campbell, J. (1981). *Myths to live by: An interview.* New York: Educational Broadcasting Corporation.

Emerson, E W., & Forbes, W. E. (1909-14). *The journals of Ralph Waldo Emerson* (10 volumes). Boston: Houghton Mifflin.

Hunt, D. (1987). *Beginning with ourselves: In practice, theory, and human affairs.* Toronto: OISE Press.

Maynes, F. J., & Ross, J. (1985). Growth in the appreciation of literature. *Orbit, 16*(4), 9-12.

Miller, J. P. (1983). *The educational spectrum: Orientations to curriculum.* New York: Longman.

Miller, J. P. (1986). Atomism, pragmatism, holism. *The Journal of Curriculum and Supervision, 1*(3), 175-196.

Miller, J. P. (1987). Transformation as an aim of education. *The Journal of Curriculum Theorizing, 7*(1), 94-152.

Miller, J. P. (1988). *The holistic curriculum.* Toronto: OISE Press.

Miller, J. P., & Seller, W. (1985). *Curriculum, perspectives and practice.* New York: Longman.

Ontario Ministry of Education. (1986). *History and contemporary studies.* Toronto: Ministry of Education.

Ontario Ministry of Education. (1988). *Geography: Intermediate and senior divisions.* Toronto: Ministry of Education.

Ontario Ministry of Education. (1988). *Growing with books. Children's literature in the formative years and beyond: Resource guide.* Toronto: Author.

Park, P. (1983). Integrated approach to social education: Environmental studies. In J. Parsons, G. Milburn, & M. van Manen (Eds.), *A Canadian social studies.* Edmonton, Alberta: University of Alberta.

Samples, B. (1976). *The metaphoric mind: A celebration of creative consciousness.* Reading, MA: Addison Wesley.

Sanders, D., & Sanders J. A. (1983). *Teaching through metaphor: An integrated brain approach.* New York: Longman.

Schön, D. A. (1983). *The reflective practitioner: How professionals think in action.* New York: Basic Books.

Shapiro, B. (1988, November). The formation of character in schools. Unpublished speech given at the Anglican Bishops' Synod, Timmins, Ontario.

Thiessen, D. (1989, April 6). Personal correspondence.

Williams, O. (1963). *The mentor book of major British poets.* New York: New American Library.

Williams, V. L. (1983). *Teaching for the two-sided mind.* Englewood Cliffs, NJ: Prentice Hall.

CHAPTER 2

PART I:
HUMAN THEMES: DISCOVERING OUR LIFE STORY THROUGH MYTHOLOGY

INTRODUCTION

The Grade 9 English class was nearing the end of a three-week mythology unit. They had just finished a visualization exercise, called the "Wise Person Visualization," in which they had asked the advice of a wise person about a particular problem they were experiencing. One boy shared that his wise man had told him to take one step at a time as he encountered the trials and obstacles in his path. Another girl who had been physically abused in the past shared that her wise man had told her she could love someone and that she needed to be patient with herself.

The rest of the class listened in hushed silence as a few other students shared the advice they had received in the visualization. Some students saw clear pictures; others heard a voice; a few felt the experience rather than saw or heard it. When they were asked who the wise person was they discovered that each had had a unique experience. A male, female, or even an animal represented the wise person. The class discussed for a while and ultimately decided that the wise person was actually a part of themselves; a part that was connected to their true selves and spoke with their inner voices.

This mythology unit obviously went beyond the traditional Grade 9 explorations. It tapped into what was meaningful to adolescents. It also allowed a bonding process to occur in the class as individuals shared their own stories in a trusting climate.

This chapter presents an approach to mythology which connects myths to personal narratives and the personal mythologies or belief systems that are interwoven through life stories. The first part of the chapter presents a conceptual framework and academic grounding for the approach. The second part presents four levels of teaching mythology with suggested strategies for each level. The levels are designed so that as the teacher moves from one level to another there is an increasing personal connection to the material being studied.

What is a Myth?

Before the written word most societies passed stories from generation to generation by word of mouth. Today these stories are known to us as myths, and come to us from cultures that range from Ancient Greece to Mayan to Chinese to Native Canadian and American. At one level the stories are fictional and can be regarded as simply entertaining tales. Yet, the details of the stories that survived over many tellings had a more important purpose than entertainment. Many of the myths explained why certain natural phenomena occurred. Creation myths accounted for how the world began. The myth of Persephone and Demeter explained the seasons. Yet, there is still a deeper level from which one can interpret myths. Many of the stories have messages about how we can best live our lives so that they have meaning and purpose. At this level myths become stories of our search for truth and significance.

Today the stories still offer good entertainment. However, myths no longer hold valid and acceptable explanations for the physical world. Do they still contain some wisdom relevant to our daily lives? Human psyches have not changed. We still struggle with the same basic conflicts and dilemmas as did the story-teller from ancient cultures. Indeed, the same basic themes seem to be interwoven through our interpersonal and intrapersonal conflicts. We too are faced with transitions from one life stage to another, and must learn to deal with change and growth. We too undergo a quest for identity. We too experience a need for meaning and purpose in our lives.

Today, we rarely listen to stories that have been passed down through the generations. The popular media instead seems to offer a choice between innocuous but meaningless sit coms or violence-laden dramas. Joseph Campbell (1988), a noted mythologist, claims that the reason why some teenagers experience profound problems today is because there is no guiding mythology. For many young people it seems that alcohol, drugs, and promiscuous sex have replaced the stories of old in the search for meaning. Woodman (1982) concurs that addictive behaviours can, in part, be explained by the lack of a central myth. Not having a guiding mythology may be why we suffer high rates of vandalism, crime, and apathy amongst the adolescent population (Maddern, 1990).

It seems some teenagers crave "other-worldly" experiences that they induce through drugs, rebellion, and even suicide; past cultures dealt with this craving by providing other-worldly experiences through rituals (Martin, 1988). As well, the rituals celebrated growth. Ancient cultures developed initiatory experiences based on their mythologies. Today's rituals seem to be such events as passing a driver's test or coming of age to vote or drink. Only academic achievement seems to be heralded with ceremony; but these cerebral achievements rarely acknowledge the whole person. There is little community recognition when there has been a transformation of identity.

Campbell (1988) suggests that we need a new mythology that will speak to people in a modern culture in a way that offers meaning and purpose. This new mythology would address the interconnections and interdependencies among all things and provide a foundation for a global society where people live together in mutual trust. Berry (1988) believes that this new mythology must tell a new story that he calls "The Great Story of the Universe." Humans live in the context of their planet. By "storying" the scientific origins of the earth and the evolution of life on this planet, Berry believes we will feel more harmoniously connected to a larger whole and realize the responsibility we hold for the future of our earth. A new mythology, then, would show us how we have been connected to each other, animals, plants, and the beginning of time. It would guide our future. The new story would open us to transpersonal experiences of joy, love, compassion, and harmony.

As a starting point, educators can turn to the wisdom contained in the ancient mythologies for a framework for living for young people. According to Campbell, "young people just grab this stuff. Mythology teaches you what's behind literature and the arts, it teaches you about your own life. It's a great, exciting, life-nourishing subject" (1988, p. 11). Educators can also reflect on how the study of these mythologies might contribute to the creation of a modern central myth that offers wisdom to our current society.

Campbell calls educators to the task of creating a new central myth with students. Berry (1988) suggests that this new story will then guide education, shape our emotional attitudes, energize our actions, and provide us with life's purpose. Teachers have successfully taught mythology at this deeper level. Bell (1983), a practising teacher, explains why she teaches it to young adolescents:

> I teach it not only because it is the basis of Western culture, not only for the classical allusions with which one must be familiar to read the daily paper, let alone Keats and Shelley, not only for the hundreds of derivatives it has bestowed upon our language, but also to permit [adolescents] ... to participate in the universal experiences that are embodied in it. And I teach it to provide them an acceptable avenue to psychological growth and inner peace. (p. 71)

Maddern (1990) suggests that we can begin to create this new story in our schools. He examines the functions of initiation in the Aboriginal society of Australia. Initiations are times when the young are introduced to dreaming or the complex, many layered system of myth, knowledge, value, and skill that underpins Aboriginal society. He suggests that we can develop a modern curriculum that will serve the same function where students can test their own limits, "discover their strengths, learn how the world was made, find out where they fit in, recognize their responsibilities to the Earth and to society, participate actively in and with their community" (p. 13). This modern curriculum integrates disciplines and emphasizes the heart (confidence to tackle difficult emotional challenges, foster love and respect for each other), the head (organizing knowledge in an interdisciplinary fashion), and the hand (practical survival skills).

THE MONOMYTH

The myths that have survived across most cultures and over the centuries contain unmistakable similarities. Although the characters may change their appearances according to the culture, a universal pattern emerges. The structure of the story and the symbolism contained in it remain the same. In *The Hero with a Thousand Faces,* Joseph Campbell (1973) outlines the basic plot that he discovered after studying myths across different cultures. This skeleton plot repeated itself so often that Campbell came to call it the monomyth. A modified version of Campbell's monomyth is offered below as The Hero/ine's Path (Figure 2.1).

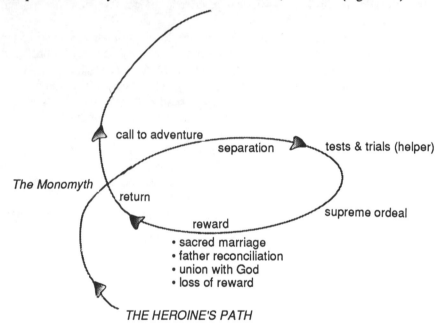

Figure 2.1

The monomyth or The Hero/ine's Path represents the basic story outline found again and again in mythology. The mythological hero/ine hears the call to adventure and is lured, carried away, or voluntarily moves toward it. Often the story involves a young man searching for his father or a way to save his kingdom. (Typically it is a male hero, a phenomena to be explored later.) After responding to the call, the hero/ine must separate from the world as he or she knows it. Inevitably there is a series of tests and trials that must be undergone. These tests may appear as demons or dragons. Often there is a "magic" helper available which the hero/ine can choose to accept or reject. According to Campbell's interpretation, after confronting many obstacles, the hero/ine faces a supreme ordeal; an obstacle that seems impossible to overcome. After successfully overcoming the supreme ordeal, the hero/ine receives the reward. The reward may be a sacred marriage (the young man marries the king's daughter), or the young man may be reunited with his father, or sometimes there is an apotheosis or union with God. In some myths the reward is lost; this is the tragic plot.

Receiving the reward is not the end of the story. Now the hero/ine must return to the world with the reward in hand. With this new identity the hero/ine must offer service to the world; he or she must in some way contribute to society the lesson learned from travelling the hero/ine's path. Campbell cautions that this stage of service is the most difficult and neglected phase of the hero/ine's journey; he also suggests that it is a most significant one.

In order to illustrate the universal pattern of the monomyth a brief synopsis of myths from five different cultures is offered below. The reader should note that, except for the Buddhist hero, Campbell's last phase of service is missing from these condensed versions.

A GREEK HERO

Perseus grew up not knowing that Zeus was really his father. His stepfather, who secretly hated him, sent him off in search of adventure and hoped to be rid of him. He went to find Medusa, a fierce Gorgon who was a terrible monster with snakes for hair. Hermes, the messenger god, acted as a helper by giving him a sword to slay Medusa. The sword acted as a mirror so that Perseus did not have to look at Medusa — for one look would turn a person into stone. He discovered Medusa's whereabouts only after stealing the one eye of the weird Gray Women. The Gray Women sent him to the three Nymphs who gave him winged shoes, a helmet that would make him invisible, and a magic wallet. After a battle with the three Gorgons, Perseus successfully cut off the head of Medusa, one of the three Gorgons. Then he discovered the beautiful Andromeda fastened by chains to a cliff by the sea. A sea monster was coming to destroy her people and only the sacrifice of her death could stop it. Perseus successfully killed the sea monster and claimed Andromeda as his bride. After this great feat he still met jealous enemies and he used Medusa's head to turn them into stone. Finally, he was able to take his mother and new wife home to Greece.

Condensed version of White (1950, pp. 27-33).

A PERSIAN HERO

Rustem, a brave 10-year-old, was declared the new hero of Iran after he killed a raging white elephant. The then empty throne of Iran was threatened by the neighbouring king. Rustem volunteered to attack the invader. First he had to tame an incorrigible, dangerous mare named Rakush. Riding Rakush, he defeated his enemy and there was peace in Iran. One day Rakush was stolen. He went to the people who had stolen his horse and threatened the King of Samenga with the death of many of his citizens. He was feasted by these people but he still could not find his horse. That night a veiled woman, the king's daughter, came to his bed and confessed her love for the handsome hero for she had heard of his many great deeds. She promised to lead him to his horse if he would marry her. They married and Rakush was returned. Then he knew he must leave for home, and so he mounted Rakush and rode home.

Condensed version of White (1950, pp. 118-133).

AN AMERICAN INDIAN HERO

Little-Man-With-Hair-all-Over was a tiny ugly man who was also very courageous. He succeeded at everything he did. In return for killing the bear monster, the grateful people gave him a magic knife. Then he met up with two travelling brothers. Little-Man killed the ugly dwarf who plagued the two brothers. Next he went down deep into the earth to examine the dwarf's home. At the entrance, he met a fierce two-headed monster and, after a savage fight, managed to cut off both of its heads with his magic knife. Then he reached another door where he met a three-headed monster and he cut off all three heads. Finally he met a monster with four heads. This challenge offered the most difficult struggle, but he managed to cut off all four heads. Then he discovered three lovely sisters who had been kept as prisoners by the monsters. He released the sisters. The two travelling brothers refused to help Little-Man climb back up the hole. Without their aid and after a great struggle, he managed to climb out of the hole. He proposed to all three sisters. So Little-Man-With-Hair-all-Over married the girls and they were very happy together.

Condensed version of Erodes and Ortiz (1984, pp. 185-191).

A BUDDHIST HERO

A young, recently decorated military prince named Prince Five Weapons began travelling with his five weapons to go home to his father. He came to the forest where Ogre Sticky-Hair lived. Ogre

Sticky-Hair killed every person he saw and the people warned the prince not to enter the forest. Undaunted, the prince entered and soon met Ogre Sticky-Hair, who threatened to eat him. The prince tried his poison arrows against Ogre Sticky-Hair but they all stuck to Ogre's hair. Next he tried his sword and then struck him with a club but both weapons stuck to his hair. Finally the prince took to attacking him with his hands, feet, and head. However, all his limbs and his head got stuck in the Ogre's hair. Ogre Sticky-Hair did not understand why the prince was still not afraid. Prince Five Weapons answered that he had a thunderbolt in his belly that would destroy the Ogre if he ate him. Ogre Sticky-Hair was afraid of death and let the prince go. The prince was in reality the future Buddha and now he preached the doctrine to Ogre Sticky-Hair who was subdued and transformed. Then the prince went home.

Condensed version of Campbell (1973, pp. 85-89).

A WEST AFRICAN HERO

Mokele had a miraculous birth as the child of the favourite wife of an African tribal chief in Zaire. As a young man his quest was to find the sun which was hidden by a far away tribe. Mokele dug out a canoe from a very large tree. Many animals came out of the forest and joined him on his voyage. This voyage included the tortoise who divined the way in the bow of the boat, and wasps who promised to sting the owners of the sun if they were not co-operative. After a long journey they arrived in the home of Mokulaka who had hidden the sun. Although Mokulaka promised to give Mokele the sun, he secretly plotted to poison Mokele. A wasp overheard the plot and told Mokele about it. Mokele decided to say nothing but to take the sun by force. The beautiful daughter of Mokulaka fell in love with Mokele. She spilled the poison and decided to run off and elope with the handsome young man. The sun was released by the tortoise. Mokele and his bride left with the boat load of animals. The warriors chased after them but were stopped by the stinging of the wasps.

Condensed version of Knappert (1986, pp. 69-73).

The Monomyth as Metaphor

The question remains as to why the same plot has continually been repeated in different stories from different cultures. It is a plot that appears to strike a universal chord. A close look at popular modern stories reveals the same basic pattern. Luke Skywalker in Star Trek, Indiana Jones, even Rambo follow the same skeleton plot. Young people playing the video game Nintendo are responding to the same story line. That the monomyth has survived over the centuries suggests that there is something in it that appeals to the psyche of all humans.

Campbell (1973, 1988) suggests that the skeleton plot offers much more than a good vehicle for a story. The journey of the hero/ine can be viewed as a metaphor for an inner journey; it can be interpreted as a metaphorical map which tells us how to successfully negotiate life transitions. Viewed as a metaphor, it becomes an archetypal journey with archetypal central themes; the journey of the hero/ine becomes universally meaningful and can be responded to across cultures. Not only is the journey undertaken by such familiar hero/ines as Theseus, Quetzalcoatl, Horus, Adonis, Persephone, Demeter, Spider Woman, Prometheus, Cybele, Bear Man, and Achilles, but it is also the journey everyone undergoes when moving from one life phase to another. Humans may not be hero/ines in the grand sense, "but essentially, everyone's story is the same. It's the story of the hero's or heroine's journey. There may be a lot of diverse things in terms of specifics, but basically we're all journeying with the same story" (Miller, 1988, p. 43).

A metaphorical interpretation of the story line might read as follows: An individual is called to adventure. This may occur because she or he initiated a change, such as starting a new job or beginning a new relationship; or the change may be thrust upon the individual by, for example, the death of a significant person or physical maturation. Now the person must separate from the familiar world and plunge into the unknown. This stage is accompanied by the grieving process that accompanies loss, and the anguish that goes with stepping into the unknown. The next stage is overcoming a series of tests or obstacles. Often these trials originate from our own negative thinking ("I can't do it. I'm not good or smart enough") or our attachment to material things ("I can't risk taking time off work to upgrade my education because I need the money to continue my current life style"). As in the myths there is usually a "magic" helper, or someone or something that will facilitate an easier journey if the hero/ine is willing to recognize and accept the help. Campbell tells us that the helper is often our own inner voice which will direct us if we choose to listen to the core of our being.

The journey, then, represents the path of personal growth. The individual treading the path is undergoing a transition from one life stage to another. This may mean a profound change; one stage must die to so that there is personal transformation or rebirth. This will be a painful struggle filled with tests and obstacles. However, these trials are a significant part of the journey as personal growth comes from either the trials themselves or the illuminating insights revealed during the trials. Pain becomes a teacher.

The reward of the journey can be no less than a transformation of consciousness. There is the joyful experience that accompanies real growth. The last stage is to completely sacrifice the old consciousness and return to the world in a new state of consciousness. It then becomes the duty of the journeyer to share new-found knowledge with the society in which she or he lives.

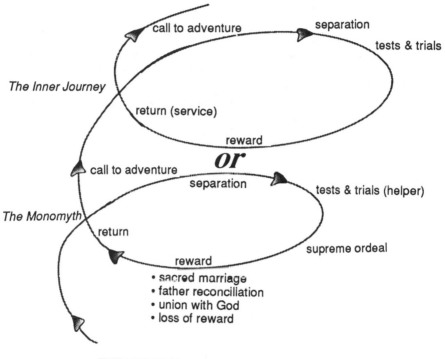

THE HEROINE'S PATH

Figure 2.2

THE INNER JOURNEY: A SPIRALLING PATH

The inner journey or growth toward wholeness can be symbolized by a cone or three-dimensional spiral (see Figure 2.2). One proceeds from one winding to the next as one successfully learns life's lessons. It is possible to move forward while frequently circling back. Often we re-circle a spiral winding as life gives us another opportunity to learn the required lessons we did not quite master. For example, we may continue to choose an unsuitable partner and have to retrace our steps until we learn to respect ourselves and choose an appropriate one. The path often is experienced as a labyrinth — a state of chaos and confusion. Like Theseus wandering lost through the labyrinth, one needs to have Ariadne's thread as a guide out of the maze into knowledge and wisdom. In *The Mystic Spiral: Journey of the Soul,* Purce (1980) develops the spiral as the symbol of human's inner journey. She points out that spirals are found in most religions and in the literature and architecture of most cultures. The spiral then seems to be an archetypal image which has universal meaning. The famous journeys of Moses, Ulysses, and Dante are examples of human's spiralling evolutionary development that have become literary classics.

The journey of awareness involves a winding path along which one proceeds toward wisdom and wholeness. Yet, it is a gentle path where each winding is a complete spiral and each spiral just a winding (see Figure 2.3). There are cycles of growth in a continuous process that never begins or ends. Moments of crisis and decision are growth junctures which mark a release from or death of one state of being and a growth or rebirth to the next state. We move onto another winding, proceeding toward another death before a rebirth.

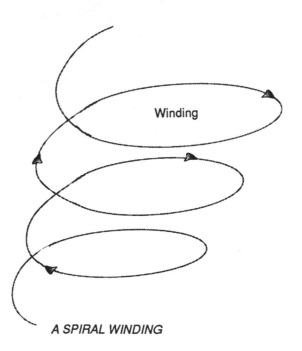

Winding

A SPIRAL WINDING

Figure 2.3

During the first part of life people are generally travelling upward and outward in spiralling windings. The spiral windings are outward as one establishes one's place in the world and achieves social status, job recognition, and material wealth. Predictable transitions an individual must make are from childhood to adolescence to young adulthood to adulthood. Predictably, an adolescent must break away from the family and accept self-responsibility.

In the second half of one's life the spiral windings tend to be inward as one passes through young adulthood to middle and old age. One has often achieved social and material success in the outer world, but is left with the question, "Is this all there is?" Typically, an individual's interests turn to a more spiritual route where one looks for how one can be of service in the world.

Individuals keep spiralling through the windings at different levels of depth, breadth, and height. As we travel our journey is rarely experienced as a linear path. It is only in looking back that we can chart the distance we have come. Often we feel that we are travelling on a path with many spirals; one woman described it as a net of interconnecting spirals; another as an experience full of space and voids; a man described his experience as a brillo pad full of tiny sharp tightly connected spirals. According to Pearson (1989), "It's not so much that we go anywhere, but that we fill out.... The journey fills us out and gives us substance. People who have taken their journeys feel bigger.... We feel the size of their souls" (p. 154).

THE LIFE STORY OR PERSONAL NARRATIVE

In the search for meaning and purpose it is important not to overlook how people make meaning of specific events in their lives. We tend to interpret our lives through the stories we tell. Our life story is our way of knowing who we are; it is our identity (McAdams, 1985). Our interpretation is temporal; it connects the past, perceived present, and the anticipated future. This pattern found in the narrative structure acts as an organizing principle and provides unity and purpose (Sarbin, 1986).

In every culture women and men pass through a series of predictable cycles of transition. These cycles are often precipitated by bodily changes and cannot be denied. It seems as if as soon as an individual has completed a transition or spiral winding she or he is thrust into the next. As one completes each spiral winding there is personal growth or a transformation of consciousness; one sees the world differently and behaves in new ways.

Other major life events could signal a time for personal growth. These events could be either positive or negative, but would act as a catalyst for growth (see Figure 2.4). Outstanding personal success, marriage, added family members, or a career change could mark a new spiral winding. On the other hand a life-threatening illness, significant personal loss, divorce, being a victim of crime or violence, or a financial change may also trigger a transition in identity that will involve personal growth.

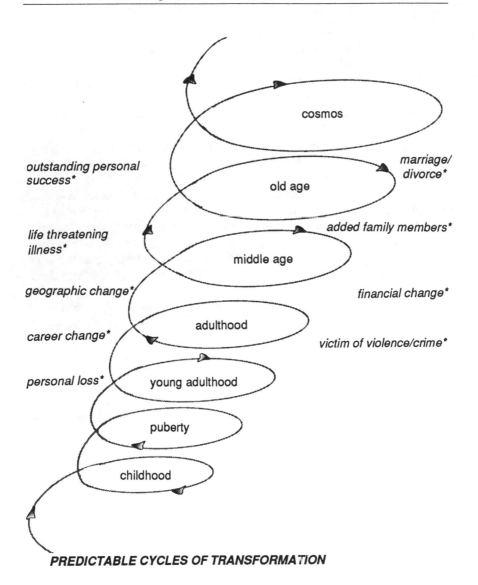

cosmos

outstanding personal
success*

old age

marriage/
divorce*

life threatening
illness*

middle age

added family members*

geographic change*

financial change*

adulthood

career change*

victim of violence/crime*

personal loss*

young adulthood

puberty

childhood

PREDICTABLE CYCLES OF TRANSFORMATION

*POSSIBLE CYCLES OF TRANSFORMATION**

Figure 2.4

The Cycles of Transformation and the Monomyth

The spiral represents cycles of change. In any transition there can be a process of transformation; a process involving personal growth. The metaphorical map of the monomyth, then, can offer another dimension of meaning. A cycle of growth can be embedded into a spiral winding; each spiral winding can be seen as following the path of the hero/ine. The skeleton plot can be simplified to three basic steps that individuals must travel through to complete a cycle of transformation. These steps can be labelled as, alternatively, death/threshold/rebirth, or separation/initiation/return, or end/middle/beginning as shown in Figure 2.5.

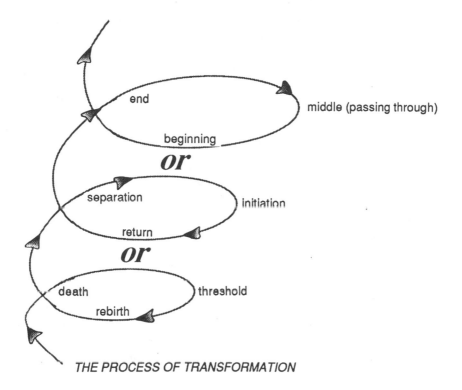

THE PROCESS OF TRANSFORMATION

Figure 2.5

Characteristically the journey involves a death of the world as it has been known, a struggle to reach the threshold of something new, and a rebirth and moving on. The pattern could also be interpreted as beginning with a separation from the known world, followed by an initiation period which must be passed through before there is a return to the world with a new identity. Yet another interpretation is that the journey consists of an ending of life as we knew it, followed by a middle or passing through, and then a new beginning.

A divorce where the husband leaves home would most likely mark the beginning of a spiral winding for a teenager. The absent father would represent the death of a family unit as the adolescent knew it, an ending. Propelled by external forces, the teenager finds herself or himself separated from life in a two-parent family. The middle or passing through is marked by the struggle of stepping into the unknown and the pain and anguish of letting go of the known.

This is the initiation period; a time leading up to reaching the threshold. It is a time when the teenager is forced to confront the tests and trials involved in actively experiencing new ways of being. Eventually the teenager accepts the new family status and personal responsibility for her or his own happiness. This is a state of rebirth; a return to the world with a new identity; a beginning.

The plot for a chapter of one's life, then, will follow the basic skeleton plot of the monomyth which incorporates the pattern of end/middle/beginning or death/threshold/rebirth. It is interesting to note that the traditional beginning, middle, and end found in most stories is paralleled by the end/middle/beginning. For example, the chapter may tell the story of a journey through a predictable life transition such as the mid-life crisis marking the beginning of middle age.

Adolescents are at the beginning of a new chapter in their life stories. They are compelled to confront the questions, "Who am I?" and "How do I fit into the adult world?" by the physical growth and changes which signify an entry into a new way of being. The adolescent is at a natural turning point which is an ideal time to recognize and reorganize the past and to bind together the past, present, and future (McAdams, 1985). According to McAdams, by this age the adolescent has developed the cognitive structures needed to construct stories which integrate the disparate parts of her or his life and provide unity and purpose.

Life stories are living and dynamic; they need to be told and retold, heard and reheard to reveal their meaning. One's identity lies in the consistency of the story as one travels through the spirals of life. Yet, real change or transition to a new spiral can only come when one revises or reconstructs the life story. That is, one interprets the story in a new way. There is a reframing of the context of the same events. The old interpretation must die so that there can be a new identity or rebirth and one can move on to the next stage of the journey.

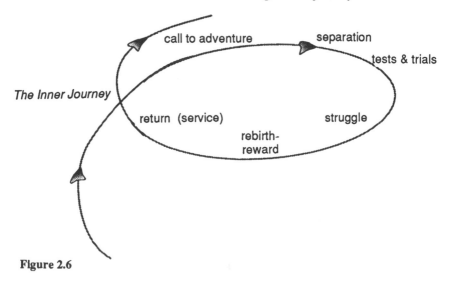

Figure 2.6

For example, a teenage girl interprets her boyfriend's obsessive jealousy as proof that he loves her. She continues on in the stormy relationship. Slowly she manages to build on her own achievements and feel a greater sense of self-worth. She reflects on her new experiences and her old story. Slowly she reconstructs the story as she understands that his jealousy showed insecurity rather than love and her own insecurity prevented her from letting go and being her own person. She has reconstructed a new story of the same events; her new interpretation allows her to either move on or build a more positive relationship with her boyfriend.

Threaded through our stories is a personal mythology that also evolves and changes. This personal mythology revolves around what one believes in and determines how one perceives oneself and one's circumstances. We are usually unaware of our own personal mythology; however, it guides and directs our behaviour. Feinstein and Krippner (1988) have described personal mythology as consisting of a number of personal myths that are either complementary or in conflict with each other. All myths are organized around one central theme by which an individual organizes experience. Personal myths evolve out of such sources as heroes and heroines of the culture; relations with teachers, parents, or significant others from the past; and positive and negative reinforcements for behaviour.

A young man may have interpreted the previous chapters of his life story with the perspective that he was not very bright and was likely to fail at most tasks. This perspective is a part of his personal mythology which not only guided his behaviour but coloured his interpretation of his story. Now the young man has discovered through the help of a supportive teacher that he actually has a lot of intellectual ability. After a series of successful experiences his personal mythology is altered and he perceives himself as capable and likely to succeed at most tasks. His life story still has unity. That is, he is still the same person and the events in previous chapters are still the same. However, his story is undergoing some major editing. He interprets the events differently and he has re-framed the context. The old story has ended. Before his failures were seen as the inevitable result of inferior intelligence. Now the failures are being perceived as a result of an inadequate concept of self. Further, the young man interprets these failures as learning experiences which helped him eventually be successful. A new story is beginning.

There is rarely a smooth or quick transition from old story to new story. We must go through the editing process of reflection and reconstruction at the same time as we experiment with new ways of being. It may seem like one step forward and two steps back. The process of reflection involves an exploration and questioning of beliefs, values, roles, relationships, and self-image. This reflection involves making the guiding personal mythology explicit. At the same time there is an active experimentation with new beliefs, values, roles, relationships, and self-image; a new personal mythology is emerging. Finally, when there is a commitment to the new mythology, there is a transformation in behaviour that is congruent with the new identity in the emerging story.

To facilitate successful transitions the student's life story can be embedded in a larger or deeper story. As students begin to understand the metaphor of the mythological map, they are able to see that their own lives may follow a similar pattern. For example, as they have experienced moving into high school or a first job or the break-up of an intense love, they have grown and changed. They have followed the pattern of end/middle/beginning. The first step is to interpret the life story in terms not only of plot, character, and theme, but also in the framework of the universal monomyth. Then students can examine the guiding personal mythology within their own stories and observe how it changes and develops as they change and develop.

This framework for viewing the life story, interwoven with a personal mythology embedded in a universal mythology, allows one to weave the disparate parts of one's experience into a meaningful whole. A larger vision can help students deal with personal crises that inevitably arise during the quest for identity. In our society crisis is viewed as a sign of sickness or weakness and is often accompanied by anxiety, loneliness, or shame. However, if crisis is viewed from a larger perspective as a time of growth, students can often experience it with excitement and anticipate social support.

Linking the life story to mythology also allows a greater vision of the future. Myths remind one that there is a reward for the struggle; the reward is personal growth. One can gain the reward only after facing and confronting the obstacles on the path to growth. One can set goals to reflect this mythic perspective, and then can act in ways to actualize the goals. Finally, reflection upon the consequences of action is possible from a larger framework than one's own necessarily limited world.

Connecting to Younger People

The journey of the hero or heroine is the archetypal journey that everyone seems to travel in the quest for self-identity. Some researchers believe that archetypes reflect a genetically coded maturational plan (Feinstein & Krippner, 1988). That is, there is an innate sequence of archetypes that guides the psychological development of an individual from birth to maturity. According to this theory, the child first associates with the Great Mother archetype which serves to connect her or him with the home and family. The hero/ine archetype later propels the adolescent away from the bonds of family and toward separation and autonomy. It is the journey of the hero/ine, then, that seems most appropriate for adolescents who are on a quest for self-identity by virtue of their developmental stage.

Following this explanation, young people are being beckoned by the call of adventure by the very nature of their biological age . The quest is to discover one's true self, one's nature, and what one should do with one's life in order to truly fulfill one's potential. This search involves a transformation, a death/threshold/

rebirth or ending/middle/beginning. To facilitate this adventure, a teacher can use the blueprint offered in The Hero/ine's Path (see p. 18) to mark the steps of the journey ahead in young peoples' quests for the meaning and purpose in their lives.

In the past, cultures had rituals and myths that acted as rites of passage which guided them through the spiral windings. For example, in earlier cultures such as that of the Plains Indians, young men were initiated into manhood through a ceremony called the Sun Dance. This ceremony was by its very nature painful and difficult, but it heralded entry into a new position in life. Symbolically the young men went through the same steps of death, struggle, and reward that life would require of them. Social support eased the transition, and a time of crisis was celebrated as a time of growth.

Today, we have few rituals to mark and celebrate the inevitable life transitions. Foster and Little, in their article "The Fasting Quest as a Modern Rite of Passage" (1988), successfully use the end/middle/beginning map when working with individuals in crisis. In a program called "Vision Quest," adapted from Native American cultures, people are offered the end/middle/beginning concept as a model for change and are sent out into the wilderness to be alone until they have resolved a personal crisis. According to Foster and Little, this model can offer a powerful rite of passage and be an important source of moral and psychological support for people going through life changes.

Formal rituals have been simulated successfully by school systems. Martin, in "Running Wolf: Vision Quest and the Inner Life of the Middle School Student" (1988), states that a few high schools currently allow "graduating seniors" to physically take a "Vision Quest" course. He suggests that a mental "Vision Quest" can be instituted for children between the ages of 11 to 14 years by the study of myths on a global basis. Students will see they are not alone in their struggles. "Indeed, a kind of pride in their struggle can develop as they begin to compare the similarity of their plight with that of say, a young Arthur Pendragon [King Arthur], Moses, Siddhartha, or even Cinderella" (p. 38). Maddern (1990) argues that we could develop a whole curriculum for 13 to 18-year-olds based on the process and functions of initiation dealt with in mythologies. This curriculum would allow students to not only tackle difficult intellectual problems, but also to cope with negative emotions. Fear and doubt could be turned into confidence, confusion into vision, anger into compassion, and greed into self-discipline.

On Resisting the Journey

It seems to be a natural human phenomenon to resist change; whether the change is positive or negative. Many people try to avoid taking the inner journey and experiencing the pain and anguish of stepping into the unknown. We try to hold onto the old because it is familiar. We fear reaching out for something we really want because we might fail. It is easier not to risk going back to school. We stay in negative relationships because the devil we know is better than the one we do not know.

Despite our resistance, life has a way of catching up with us. Our bodies change and we are thrust into adulthood, middle age, or old age. People who have been significant in our lives die or leave. Technological changes force us to adapt to new ways of being. However, when one understands the map of the inner journey it becomes clear that one is travelling on a spiral of growth; the spiral will be painful, but it will also offer a very real reward. To resist change is often just as painful and can include the pitfall of living an unfulfilled life.

We are living in an age of unprecedented change. The phenomena of marriage, divorce, and remarriage has made the nuclear family seem like the exception. Three or four career changes are commonplace. Nuclear annihilation is an everyday threat. It is easy to feel fragmented rather than whole. The young person today can expect to experience more rapid change in her of his journey than the young person of the past. They will not only have to journey through the predictable life crises as did their ancestors, but they also will probably encounter several major life events that may trigger additional spirals of growth. In addition, during adolescence important decisions must be made about such things as drugs, alcohol, and sex. These decisions can mean repeatedly going around the same spiral winding, or circling back before moving forward. Understanding the map of personal growth may facilitate a quicker, less fragmented, journey.

Young people can choose to perceive this accelerated pace of change as providing greater opportunities for growth. From this perspective it seems even more imperative that transitions be accompanied by an awareness of the inner journey. For, if the young person can apply the wisdom available through mythology to the inner journey, she or he will be grounded as she or he moves through the spiral windings. As well, if as a culture we value the map described here metaphorically, then we will support and celebrate others as they pass through the crises that indicate growth.

Teachers will often encounter students who resist taking the journey and feel stuck. Students can be encouraged to reflect on why they are behaving this way. What is holding them back? They say they would like to try a certain new venture and take a positive risk, but find themselves unable to act upon their desires. Perhaps there is a sound reason and, for them, change will not necessarily mean growth. Often, however, the support of the teacher is enough to allow the individual to move on to the next step.

HEARING THE INNER VOICE

Stories in mythology have been passed down through the ages because they speak to the hearts and reveal the inner voice of generation after generation. Whether it is the story of an Indian healer, a Grecian god or goddess, or the Buddha, the similarities of the stories speak a universal language. It is a universal language of metaphor and symbol which is difficult to speak of in any terms other than the parable. The inner voice is Ariadne's thread which can guide one out of the chaos of the labyrinth of life and into clarity and light. The voice speaks a wisdom available to all, a wisdom from deep within the heart. It is sometimes called intuition or a direct knowing, coming from some place other than the inquiring mind.

How can one gain access to intuition or to the inner voice? It comes in a language that is best understood in a relaxed state with an accepting frame of mind. In the classroom students can learn to hear their own inner voices by being quiet first. Teachers can teach physical relaxation exercises and guide imagery sessions. Students can learn to listen to the intuition of the body which speaks its own truth when one becomes aware of it. If students are still enough they can learn to listen to the core of their being, or "the message from the heart." And finally, mythology offers a map, a reference point which can be used to determine where we are on the path of personal growth.

Each individual must follow her or his own path. The path to fulfilling one's potential is unique to each person and involves discovering what makes one deeply happy. It is a "path with heart." Joseph Campbell (1988) refers to this as "Follow your bliss." The key to discovering one's bliss is learning to listen to the heart or inner voice; the means lies in doing what makes one truly happy. For example, if a student knows in her or his heart that working at a medical career is what brings true satisfaction, then this, rather than working in the family business as expected, is the "path with heart." Once the student has discovered what experiences are "blissful" mythology tells her or him to stay with this regardless of external opinions. The teacher then should not be externally commanding with "shoulds," but rather be the facilitator of a student following her or his own inner voice. Adolescents armed with this philosophy appear to be able to take more positive risks with their lives.

The God/dess

One does not have to look far in the study of mythology to recognize the sexism inherent in it. The journey is essentially the journey of the hero. The young man goes out into the world to find his destiny. The female docilely minds the hearth, waiting for the prince to rescue her. The reward for the male who successfully comes through his trials is marriage. For the female, the marriage is usually the beginning of her trials (Weigle, 1982). These are hardly ingredients that will speak positively to female students and strengthen their self-images. Yet, the map for inner growth that the great archetypal stories provide is as relevant for females as it is for males. The hero myth moves us toward the highest development of autonomy and individuality. It refers to "the primary task of the first half of life [as] an inward task for us all and has nothing to do with being male or female" (Olds, 1981, p. 177).

The question then becomes, how can a teacher address mythology and encourage a vision of a strong female. As the entry point, the teacher can introduce a myth in terms of what it tells us about the culture in which it originated. The

sexism found in myths across the cultures is generally reflected by the construction of a powerful male and a dependent female. Historically, this has been
portrayed as the relative position between the sexes, and myths and their symbols
have been designed to perpetuate these positions (Ruether, 1985). This approach
also helps explain the violence in myths as emerging from male-dominated
societies that have a generally hierarchic and authoritarian structure with a high
degree of social violence evidenced particularly in the form of warfare (Eisler,
1987).

But mythology has not always been told from a patriarchal perspective.
One interpretation of primordial myth is that there was a Great Goddess, mother
earth, who created and governed the world. She was identical to the universe
itself. Great Mother Goddess gave birth to the goddesses and gods and sent divine
laws to her prophets. Under her rule the earth enjoyed a long period of peaceful
progress and society was based largely on agriculture. Eisler cites the work of
University of California archaeologist Marija Gimbutus (1982) as revealing
evidence that this type of life was a reality not a fiction.

However, by 1750 BC, matriarchal societies had been crushed by large
scale invasions perpetuated by aggressive males. Wars, violence, and chaos
prevailed. The Goddess' power was usurped violently by a stern and vengeful god
like Zeus or Yahweh. The reign of male supremacy had begun, and the subsequent
myths reflected this perspective. The myths were designed to prevent women
from being independent of men, earning their own money or making their own
choices for mating. The patriarchal culture was perpetuating its own values.

Viewed first in this historical and sociological context, myths can hopefully be examined with a critical awareness. Female students can recognize a
myth's shortcomings in offering female models for living, and still profit from the
valuable lessons the myth has to offer. In *The Chalice and the Blade,* Eisler (1987)
weaves evidence from art, archeology, religion, social science, history, and many
other fields of inquiry into new patterns that tell a "new story" of our cultural
origins. She takes into account the whole of human history (including prehistory)
as well as the whole of humanity (both its female and male halves). Eisler offers
this new story or reframing of history, which leads to new ways of structuring
politics, economics, science, and spirituality, as a partnership between male and
female. Exploring this new story of our cultural origins can incorporate many
different subject areas and allows students a different sense of place in their own
lives and in history. This can help them create new patterns of meaning as to who
they are and where they are in the grand sense of things. It also allows for a new
way to anticipate the future.

There seems to be an age-old, love-hate conflict with the feminine aspect
in mythology. Examining this love-hate conflict may shed light on modern gender
issues. Mythologically, it is the woman who gives birth to all things. She is truly
loving and compassionate. Through the feminine nature comes acceptance of the
natural cycles of sexuality, birth, and death. And it is the woman who holds the

thread of wisdom, who has access to intuitive knowing. It is the female that represents the mystery of life, the unknown.

Yet, it is the female who brings us into this world and introduces us to pain and suffering. Woman has been linked with evil since the Garden of Eden. And it is archetypal woman who is held responsible for man's downfall. In myths from the Golden Age of Greece and Rome, to the Garden of Eden of the Christians and Jews, it is the female who causes a fall from paradise and an ending of dismal failure. "It is not much of a step at all from the initial image of Adam and Eve to a belief in woman's inferiority, and her inevitable involvement in evil and earthly dimensions, with man as a superior, purer creature, whose only error was to be corrupted by a sinful Eve" (Olds, 1981, p. 146).

The teacher should also make a conscious effort to present students with myths that do portray a strong female. Joseph Campbell (1973) concurs that the hero/ine can be male or female. The fact that he offers 49 male heroes and only 12 female heroines indicates that the task of choosing a strong female will require effort. The strong female stories Campbell included were Leda and Helen, Cybele, Virgin Mary, Joan of Arc, Pluades (Australian Aboriginal), Penelope, Persephone and Demeter, Wanjiru (African), Inanna or Ishtar, and Hiiaka (Polynesian). Campbell (1988) suggests that mythologically the heroine's journey can consist of the female being transformed from a maiden to a mother. She goes through the ordeal of pregnancy and childbirth to bring back the child as a reward to the world. Yet it seems that a woman is capable of much more than a journey dictated by biology. Noble (1990) believes that the essence of women's heroic quest is pursuing great possibilities which seem beyond what is believed achievable.

According to Noble, the journey of the hero encourages the male hero to be a successful warrior who displays exceptional strength and/or sociopolitical power. He displays autonomy, courage, independence, intelligence, creativity, integrity, self-control, and lives life according to his own terms regardless of the cost. On the other hand, the heroine learns to cultivate her beauty and purity, to sublimate her desire for autonomy, growth, and adventure, and to find her identity through her relationship with a man. Noble believes instead that the myths should encourage females to be heroes instead of heroines and that as a result women will experience the struggles of the journey differently.

Noble agrees with the hero/ine's path described in this chapter but interprets the journey from a strictly feminine perspective. "To live heroically a woman must belong to herself alone: she must be the center of her own life. She must pursue and attain a state of wholeness of authenticity which is fluid, inclusive and interconnected, and which does not preclude relationships" (p. 7). The hero will hear and may choose to heed the call to adventure. Her life will collapse in some vital way; for example: a relationship falters, a job fails to materialize, she cannot find community with others, or she loses someone, something, or some important part of herself. If she does heed the call she will be plunged into the initiation stage. For Noble, the journey necessarily involves making her way in the world of men at the same time as she must express and define her true identity as a woman. To maintain her integrity, authenticity, creativity, and independence she must take control of her life and refuse to be a victim even if there are social expectations to play that role. She must have a dream or vision for her future. Finally, she must learn to rely on her own inner strength rather than identifying with and relying on anyone else.

Along the path the hero will enter the realm of ordeal, chaos, emptiness, and even despair. It is in this realm that she will experience and must confront dragons. The first dragon is her own self. She will be tempted to go back to familiar ways of relating to the world. She must persevere even when she wants to give up; she must live through the pain. The second dragon is the voice of those who tell her to stay home and be silent and good. Here she will have to dare to speak in her own voice even as others may denounce her as shrill, shrewish, or unfeminine. The third dragon is the voice of any culture which tells women they are inferior because they are female. They must move beyond being too stupid, fat, old, poor, and/or weak to achieve their dreams. The fourth dragon is their socialized tendency to drift until someone or something rescues them, or to underdevelop their full potentials. "Independence for women is hard won. The need for love and social approval can all too easily de-self the hero" (Noble, 1990, p.14). When women become heroes they confront these deadly dragons and rid themselves of them.

The final challenge is the transformation. The hero has a new identity and a more mature self will emerge and be integrated with her younger and more fragile self. She will have freed herself from internalized misogyny, self-denial, and the sacrifice of herself to others' expectations, and be free to express her authenticity. She has come to terms with living with ambiguity and uncertainty and the fact that she may not always be successful. When she dares to live this true self publicly and fearlessly she will be giving service by acting as a role model for other women and transforming the institutions she works in. She can now serve others through caring, compassion, and recognizing the heroic potential in everyone she meets.

It seems that Noble sees one long life journey from dependence to independence. According to the framework offered in this chapter, young women could be seen as travelling on a many spiralled path which leads in the direction that Noble offers as an end point. Noble does not advocate a male clone as hero; rather she sees the female hero as being a new archetype. Her description of the female archetypal hero seems worthy of the male hero as well. The hero becomes

> independent without alienating herself from others, courageous without being contemptuous of the weak, powerful without dominating or exploiting others, rational without compromising feeling or intuition, autonomous without abjuring others; nurturing without denying her own

self; and androgynous without sacrificing the best attributes of her femaleness. (p. 8)

Although the female hero may experience the journey in a qualitatively different manner, we are all on the journey toward being all that we can be. The quest should embrace and affirm full humanity for all.

Most importantly, there is a potential heroine in every woman. Ideally, she should be the leading lady of her own life and be shaped by the choices she makes as she encounters difficulties along life's path, rather than by expectations engendered by her socialization. Choice is the operative word; if she chooses to act, to as great an extent as possible, in ways that are consistent with her values and feelings rather than someone else's, she is acting as the heroine — as the protagonist of her own myth (Bolen, 1984). In the words of Bolen, "In the process of living from this premise, something happens: a woman becomes a choice-maker, a heroine who shapes who she will become" (p. 278).

In the final analysis it is unfortunate, but telling, that myths have such a masculine perspective. The teacher cannot ignore this situation. However, this one-sidedness can be used as an opportunity to begin to set the record straight. The female of today is on her own journey of which she is the protagonist. Students can be encouraged to reconstruct the ancient mythologies with strong female personalities. Classes can construct narratives of the modern heroine who is both strong and breaks out of her subordinated position. Exploring this theme could be a part of any subject area that explores gender issues. Both male and female students can synthesize the strengths of what have traditionally been defined as the masculine and feminine aspects of themselves in their life stories. As a final challenge, the female student can be seen as a part of this age's struggle to create a relevant central myth.

BEYOND THE MONOMYTH

This chapter has focused on the journey of the hero/ine as a cycle which is particularly significant to adolescents on a quest for identity. Although the journey described here is typical, it may not fit a specific individual's experience. However, most students will identify and benefit from exploring their life story from this perspective.

There are also other valuable ways to explore the idea of metaphorical maps for growth. Some researchers believe that the archetypes we respond to are developmental and coded in our DNA (Feinstein & Krippner, 1988; Houston, 1987). Pearson (1986) offers five different archetypal journeys that she believes are developmental in nature. For Pearson, each journey offers a very positive lesson as a reward. These lessons include overcoming denial, and developing autonomy, assertiveness, confidence, courage, respect, joy, abundance, acceptance, faith, and an ability to give. Using the dragon as a symbol for the supreme ordeal, Pearson describes how each archetypal journeyer would approach this obstacle differently. The Orphan denies the dragon or waits for rescue; the Martyr sacrifices the self to it to save others; the Wanderer flees; the Warrior slays the dragon; the Magician incorporates and affirms it.

Although this journey is presumably developmental in nature, Pearson suggests that males may take their journeys in a different sequence than females. This difference could provide for interesting classroom discussion and reflections on gender issues. In exploring these differences students can become aware of alternative paths of growth and understand their own journeys better. Literature and history offer abundant examples of the variations in journeys. Subject areas concerned with building self-concept could explore these alternative paths so that students can match their own experience with that of someone else. History and politics offer non-fictional stories in which students can recognize characters on different journeys and see how they experience and resolve conflict with each other. From an environmental studies perspective, students could explore how each of these journeyers might behave toward the environment. Then, in creating the "new story," the potential contributions to the planet of each type of journeyer could be examined.

Another enriching way to learn about ourselves and others is by examining the mythological archetypal *personalities* and their relationships with others. In *Goddesses in Everywoman* (Bolen, 1984) and *Gods in Everyman* (Bolen, 1989) several goddesses and gods from Greek mythology are explored for their main personality characteristics. For example, Athena is the goddess of wisdom and craft who is ruled by her head rather than her heart. Zeus is the all-powerful male god who crushes others in his bid for power. Given that these personalities are apparently archetypal, it is likely that they can offer meaningful portraits of both ourselves and people we know and relate to. Most of us have encountered an Athena or Zeus in our day, or we may recognize an aspect of our own personality in their characters.

Knowing the goddesses and gods as archetypes helps us understand both ourselves and others better. "When knowledge of the mythic dimension comes into your possession it can help you find your bearings and a path that is true for you: one that reflects who you authentically are, which makes life meaningful" (Bolen, 1989, p. 286). Bolen suggests that we all have many gods and goddesses within us, but that we tend to resemble some more than others; however, we can activate other gods or goddesses if the situation calls for it.

As students begin to understand different personality types, they can deal with them more effectively in personal, social, and school situations. Characters from both literature and history can flesh out the archetypes. The arts can help make personality characteristics come alive and become more meaningful. Subject areas concerned with people and human nature — such as family studies, business, politics, and sociology — can all be connected to this theme.

Another human theme that could be explored is that of conflict. Mythology tells us that conflict is often experienced as tension between two existing opposites or dualities. Examination of this conflict illustrates that both of the opposites are necessary for the conflict to exist at all. For example, a teenager seeking independence shifts back and forth between dependence and independence. According to Campbell (1988), the resolution of this type of conflict comes through integration and synthesis. A review of the natural world could provide more understanding of this viewpoint. The universe, for example, is undergoing simultaneous contraction and expansion; the universe has both a violent and harmonious aspect to it. Berry (1988) suggests that we have to accept both aspects and understand and enter into the violent aspect as well as the harmonious. He claims that without this tension between chaos and harmony we cannot have creativity.

Students could explore this hypothesis of conflict and ask: Does nature offer the pattern for human nature? Can humans be creative only with the tension of opposites? Can we resolve conflict through integration and synthesis? Does one's personal narrative fit this experiential pattern? History and literature could be explored to examine the hypothesis.

Finally, global dilemmas could be explored through this hypothesis of conflict. A dilemma, by definition, is an argument forcing one to choose one of two unfavourable alternatives. However, through integration and synthesis we can perhaps reach a positive resolution. Gorbachev seems to be adopting this philosophy in his political dealings. The Berlin Wall coming down symbolizes a move towards integration of two seeming opposites, the East and the West. Environmental concerns can be explored through the same lenses. We can destroy and create simultaneously by replenishing stocks while we fish from our waters, and by planting at the same time as we cut down trees. Reconciling dualities in this manner can lead to a workable policy of resource management.

Campbell believes that educators today are in a position to begin creating a new myth with students. This is a myth of the planet; a myth that speaks to the interdependence among all things and emphasizes caring, compassion, peace, and harmony. Berry (1988) believes that to tell the complete story of anyone we have to tell the story of the universe and the individual's place in it. We need to tell the story of such things as our own community, the vegetation, rivers, waters, insects, animals, and how the natural world speaks to us. In order to be whole we need to see ourselves in the context of our environment; we cannot be well on an ill planet. Clearly the new myth must take a global perspective that is interdisciplinary and has a particular emphasis on science and the environment.

PART II: MYTHOLOGY IN THE CLASSROOM

CONNECTING ACROSS SUBJECT DISCIPLINES

As we engage in a mythical journey we struggle with insights into what it means to be human. We deal with human themes that are timeless; the power of myth lies in the universal application of these themes. Myths offer a different way of looking at the world where "all is interrelated, important to be witnessed and seen within the context of the whole" (Olds, 1981, p. 151). In the classroom we can approach the whole through making connections among subject areas.

It is, perhaps, clearest how the study of myth falls into the area of the arts. Myths can be explored as stories in their own right. Literature can be examined for its use of mythologies. Modern offerings of the media can be evaluated through this lense. Myth can be a springboard to creative writing and to understanding the universal appeal of art and music. The stories lend themselves naturally to the development of dramatic techniques. History offers a wonderful avenue from which to examine how historical heroes and heroines have travelled the hero/ine's path. The actual locations of the journeys in ancient mythologies can be charted on a modern map in geography.

The process of metamorphosis in the biological world shows that profound changes in the lives of many organisms is a natural and necessary part of their development. This process can be paralleled to the pattern in the human journey. In order for transformation to occur there has to be a death of the old before there can be a rebirth of the new. In terms of the chapters in a life story this can be seen as an end/middle/beginning or death/threshold/rebirth.

Science can offer a wonderful vehicle for experiencing the connection between ourselves and the environment. The increasingly serious nature of the global environmental crisis reinforces the necessity of environmental education. The warning signs are everywhere: resource depletion, drought, desertification, famine, and talk of the greenhouse effect. Education can play a part in reshaping the thinking and attitudes of the next generation toward the environment. Clark (1989) suggests that environmental education is not just another subject to add to an already overcrowded curriculum. He believes that "environment" needs to be understood as the entire context of our lives — as the interconnectedness among biology, technology, and culture. Environmental education must be seen as the larger picture that gives meaning to all studies. For example, if we are to re-conceptualize environmental education as an integrative study, it is necessary to understand the relationship between ecology and economics. Our capitalistic system is continually destroying our life support system in the name of economic growth. Ever increasing consumption which is dependent upon ever increasing exploitation of resources ignores the interconnection between ecology and economics. According to Clark, "If one wishes to manage the household, one must first understand how the household works. That this is not the case is evident" (p. 61).

Careful observation of the cycles of the natural world can inspire a sense of being a part of a system much larger than ourselves. Students can participate in the seasons by such hands-on activities as planting or harvesting. These types of activities can enhance students' sense of awe for the mystery of the universe; they can begin to hear nature's "voices." They can go out into the environment and quietly listen to the actual sounds of nature such as the wind whistling through the trees or the birds singing. By listening to the "voices" of nature we are better able to hear our own inner voices (Berry, 1988). *How Nature Works,* by Michael Cohen (1988), offers many experiential exercises which connect human nature to mother nature.

Given the universality of mythology, it is easy to see how it can be applied to many subject areas. For example, the hero/ine's path as a metaphorical map for the inner journey has been used in environmental studies. Students on a field trip into a remote northern community were thrust into situations where they confronted "personal firsts" such as being in a new environment, leaving home, and having to adjust to living with a new group of people. For most it was a call to adventure. The written assignment was to chart one's journey and compare it to the map of the monomyth.

True mastery of a physical skill can also take a student through the lessons inherent in the hero/ine's journey. A physical education instructor could turn to *Acrobats of the Gods: Dance and Transformation* (Blackmer, 1989) to see how the inner journey model has been applied to teaching dance. Blackmer's basic thesis is that anyone undergoing a physical training process is working on her or his concept of Self. The pain and labour involved in rigorous training can give birth to an enhanced awareness of Self.

Any subject area which includes the development of self-esteem in its objectives can utilize the model of personal growth offered in myth. Health education and family studies are two areas where growth is an explicit objective in the curriculum. The personal narrative can be embedded in the mythological framework as it connects to subject areas. Modern initiation rites involving symbolic enactments, explorations, and celebrations of the stages of a person's journey can be dramatically intensified by using poetry, music, song, mask, costume, and dance (Maddern, 1990).

Finally, comparative religion is also an excellent place to examine these concepts. It is interesting to note that the journeys of Jesus, Mohammed, Buddha, and Krishna tend to follow the same pattern as that of the monomyth. To examine these lives in this light is not meant to reduce religion to the level of myth, but rather to facilitate recognition of the connections between all persons and faiths.

MYTHOLOGY AND TEACHER ORIENTATION

The universal applicability of mythology makes it a powerful vehicle for connecting the arts and sciences to our own life stories. The ways in which this vehicle can be approached and used is limited only by the teacher's imagination. However, the teacher's position on the function of curriculum will influence the approach taken. The practical strategies offered in the second half of this chapter look at three different approaches to teaching mythology and integrated studies: through transmission, transaction, or transformation. The strategies are intended to be interdisciplinary and interconnected. Activities undertaken in isolation may appear simplistic or trivial if not placed in a larger context. The teacher can select those strategies with which she or he is comfortable.

Transmission. The objective of the teacher is to transmit facts and information while promoting culturally acceptable social values. A class studying the myth of Theseus would be given structured questions to elicit factual answers on character, plot, setting, mood, and theme. Students could then write a personal myth that has all the ingredients evident in the story of Theseus. A student's story or parts of it could be used to learn how a dramatist could best use the material in the myth of Theseus.

The fall of the Cretan civilization was a consequence of the eruption of Mount Santorini in Knosus; the palace of Minos was destroyed by volcanic activity. The fact that King Minos' palace and throne have since been discovered could lead to a historical study of the archaeological dig in Knossus. A geographical study of the floor of the Mediterranean Sea would broaden the understanding of this time in history. The study of volcanic activity and related phenomena such as tsunami would add a science component. Mediterranean music could be studied and the prescribed steps of the popular folk dances taught. Cretan art and frescoes might be studied, and the students could build a diorama of a palace in a shoe box.

Transaction. This orientation centers around the inquiry process. The process is much like a treasure hunt where students hunt for solutions by formulating hypotheses, gathering data, testing the hypotheses and then reformulating them. Traditionally, the inquiry process has been based on the scientific method which involves problem identification, problem analysis, generating alternatives, selecting a solution, implementing the solution, and evaluating it.

In teaching mythology the teacher can issue a challenge and the students can respond by applying a problem-solving method. For example, after having the class read the myth of Theseus, the teacher could challenge the students to find themselves in 1500 BC on the Isle of Crete. Violent volcanic eruptions, earthquakes and tidal waves are rocking the Mediterranean world. What would students do given the alternatives available at the time? In utilizing a problem-solving method as individuals or in groups, students would need to explore areas of history, geography, and science.

Embedded in the map of the monomyth is a problem-solving strategy that students may wish to utilize. The "call to adventure" indicates a problem that needs to be solved. Aware of the end/middle/beginning model, the problem solver must decide what the rebirth state will look like when actualized. This is the first step in the problem-solving process and involves creating a vision embedded with appropriate values and beliefs. The first steps involve endings of the old as one initiates new behaviour. The endings will be accompanied by feelings of loss. Typically people will try to hold onto the familiar. Explicit plans should be made for what has to end and strategies explored for how to deal with loss and resistance. Next one can plan for the dragons that one can see on the path ahead and develop strategies to surmount these obstacles. Some tests and trials will be particular to each situation, but in every situation predictable obstacles, to varying degrees, will include the anxiety of moving into the unknown, living with ambiguity, and reduced performance as people try new behaviours. Support systems and creating a positive environment for risk-taking begin to address these obstacles. The last stage will be the actualization or rebirth. The problem solvers can plan celebrations because the problem has been solved in a way that honours the values held by those involved in the change. Planned rewards are an important aspect of this model. Without rewards people may return to their old ways of doing things. Finally, the problem solvers need to consider how they will render service to their community. This often happens by sharing with others how they successfully solved the problem at hand.

Following this model students may work on school-based problems such as how to increase school spirit. In looking at the rebirth stage they can see the school as it ideally would be when it is infused with school spirit. In diagnosing the present state of the school and planning for action to increase school spirit, students can explicitly state what must end and plan for the obstacles ahead. For example, a short lunch hour may have to be lengthened so that students have time to be involved in school activities. At the same time the school day becomes longer. It is likely that the students and staff will resist the change as they are familiar with the short lunch hour and like going home early. Brainstorming will allow students to recognize and develop strategies to help overcome such obstacles. In addition, bus schedules will need to be changed and co-ordinated with other schools in the system. The sense of anxiety as students and staff begin to pursue new noon-hour activities needs to be anticipated and support offered. Finally, when school spirit has increased the school should plan a formal ritual to celebrate success and reinforce the new behaviours. The students' service to the community could take the form of sharing with others the problem-solving model used.

Transformation. This orientation emphasizes meaning and purpose. Mythology offers a blueprint for transformation which tells us that the journey will be difficult and painful, but that it is the only way we can grow. The path travelled is a "path with heart," meaning that the individual treading the path should feel that this is what she or he should be doing and that the path offers meaning and purpose to her of his existence. The path with heart feels right and true. There is no uncertainty that this is the right direction. This certainty does not circumvent the necessary tests and trials that one must encounter. It does not take away the pain of loss and anxiety. It does, however, add a sense of determination to continue on rather than to resist and stay behind. Individuals can look to the rebirth stage for their vision for a better self. Embedded in this vision are personal values that are important to the individual. Trusting the journey of transformation one can plan for the knowns ahead. In any transformation of identity the knowns include endings and a sense of loss, anxiety about stepping into the unknown, uncertainty of the territory ahead, and joy of reaching the rebirth stage. The service stage can also be recognized as most important and acted upon.

An in-depth examination of the myth of Theseus may offer a model for the teacher interested in the transformation approach. The origins of the violent aspect of the myth can be addressed and explanations offered, but centrally the story can be examined metaphorically as a message for personal transformation. There are really two spiral windings in the myth which exemplify that when one completes one journey one simply goes on to the next. In the first journey, Theseus is called to adventure when he finds the sword and sandals of his father who was unknown to him. He sets out on a quest to find his father. He meets a series of robbers on the road whom he successfully slays. Then he avoids certain death by strapping the wicked Procrustes to his own bed and stretching him. (Theseus has two helpers: an iron club gleaned from the first robber he met and the whispered confidence of Procrustes' servant.) Finally, he returns to the Athenian society to take his rightful place as son of the king.

In the second story, the call of adventure beckons Theseus when he learns of the terrible punishment being inflicted on his countrypeople because of an indiscretion of his father. Theseus volunteers to be one of the 14 youths to be sacrificed to the Minotaur. In order to escape death, he must kill the Minotaur and find his way out of the labyrinth in which the monster is kept. Ariadne, King Minos' daughter, acts as Theseus' helper and sneaks him a sword to kill the Minotaur and a ball of thread to retrace his footsteps out of the labyrinth. After successfully negotiating his trials, Theseus received the reward of marriage to Ariadne. On his return home, he becomes not only a hero citizen but he must take on the role of king because of his own father's untimely death.

The myth of Theseus is a splendid vehicle for illustrating how the mythological map can be a metaphor for the inner journey of personal growth. Some suggested archetypal meanings for Theseus' adventures are offered here. First, he was on a "father quest," which is a symbol of the search for one's personal identity. The trials and ordeals that Theseus encountered are really the obstacles one must face while undergoing change. Often these trials are self-created by negative attitudes and unnecessary attachments. The labyrinth or maze represents the confusion and chaos one experiences travelling through the change process. Theseus had to go to the center to slay the Minotaur. The center represents the inner voice; it is at the center that one can hear the wisdom of the inner voice. It is from the center, then, that one can best battle obstacles. Discovering his father meant Theseus had discovered his own identity and could then become a man fulfilling his own potential. The death of his father meant Theseus had to extend his personal responsibility to caring for others in the society by succeeding him as the new king.

Students are able to understand and appreciate the concepts that are involved at this level. They are interested in the conscious and the subconscious mind and the possibility of archetypes. Teachers can introduce the theory of archetypes as a possible explanation for the fact that the journey of the hero/ine exists across mythologies of most cultures. Students can also be told that visualization, dreams, and meditation are ways to tap into the Self or inner voice. They can understand and have experienced a "gut feeling"; examination of this gut feeling is a good way to introduce listening to the inner voice.

CLASSROOM APPROACHES

A suggested conceptual framework for teaching mythology as a map of the inner journey contains four levels from which a teacher may approach the lessons and experiential exercises (see Figure 2.7). The levels are seen as developmental and become increasingly personal. Strategies also tend to move from the transmission through transaction to transformation orientation. The orientations are seen to be embedded in each other in a nested relationship much like Chinese boxes. The teacher could teach the content of myth through a transmission approach, and also offer a problem-solving component utilizing a transactional approach. As well, the teacher can approach myth from the transformational orientation by exploring myths as stories which can help us construct meaning and purpose in our lives. Teaching from one orientation does not preclude the others, and activities and ideas from one level can be introduced and integrated into other levels if the teacher believes the students are ready.

An example of this nested concept is observable in the use of the mythological map for problem solving. From a transactional perspective, the student can problem solve using The Hero/ine's Path as a method of inquiry. However, the student can extend this problem-solving map to include personal transition. The student follows the same steps as in the transactional problem solving, but personal meaning is added when the student approaches the path as a path with heart. This means that the student listens to her or his inner voice and uses a benchmark such as "following one's bliss" as a guide along the path. Another element of meaning is added when the student arrives at the rebirth stage and recognizes it is time to offer service; the student must share with others what she or he has learned.

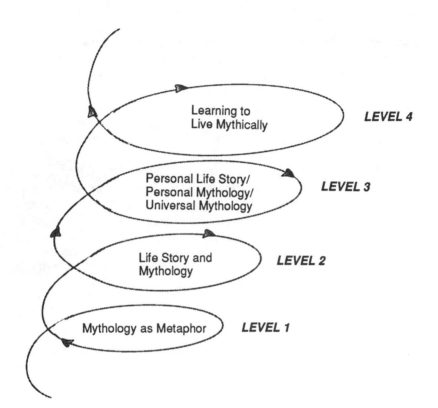

Learning to
Live Mythically   *LEVEL 4*

Personal Life Story/
Personal Mythology/   *LEVEL 3*
Universal Mythology

Life Story and   *LEVEL 2*
Mythology

Mythology as Metaphor   *LEVEL 1*

SUGGESTED DEVELOPMENTAL TEACHING SEQUENCE

Figure 2.7

Mythology as Metaphor — Level 1

The objective of this level is to have the student acquire an understanding of mythology as a metaphor for the inner journey of personal growth. For a true understanding of this the student must become familiar with the basic skeleton plot that underlies the journeys of the heros and heroines. As mentioned earlier, Joseph Campbell (1973) has identified this skeleton plot as the monomyth. A modified version of Campbell's diagram of the journey was offered in Figure 2.1.

To begin, teachers could choose to look at modern films and stories that the students identify as meaningful to them. Narrowing the field to adventure-type stories, students can compare plot lines, themes, and characters. It is during this comparison that students will probably come to a basic form of the archetypal plot of the hero/ine's journey. The teacher can add the labels that fit Campbell's terminology. The key factor that interests students here is that the character has undergone a major change in personality. From stories of their own choice they see that there will be scars, but that the hero/ines have learned lessons from the painful trials they have undergone.

Teachers can then direct students to different ancient mythologies which have incorporated the skeleton plot of what Campbell labelled the monomyth. Then students can look for similarities in ancient mythologies from different cultures and contemporary literature or film. Archetypal themes other than the hero/ine's journey can be examined. Themes such as independence, betrayal, or pride are portrayed in both mythology and relevant modern stories.

At this level, the student is asked to make a personal connection with the myths. This is a non-threatening level where students can project themselves into a part of a theme without having to risk self-disclosure or self-exploration. However, by participating, students are unconsciously identifying with the process involved in the quest for identity, and are vicariously experiencing what young people have been experiencing since the beginning of time (Bell, 1983). For example, in "Mythology and Maturation," Dell outlines a short story lesson which she claims carries with it great potential for emotional release and development as a vicarious experience. Students read the Greek myth of Phaeton and then brainstorm about ways in which teenagers who drive their father's Sun Chariot to a disastrous end could be paralleled to a modern day setting. As a class they flesh out the skeletal plot of the archetypal drama which is played out in the ancient myth. Phaeton has grown up in a fatherless home. When father and son are reunited, it is the perfect time for Phaeton to ask for a chariot. Against his better judgment Apollo gives in to the request. In this story Phaeton asserts himself prematurely. The journey of the hero/ine is not played out.

Students then write a modern day story using the skeletal plot. They can externalize problems in their own lives by projecting them onto fictitious characters. Students vicariously resolve the age-old dilemma of the need for a daughter or son to be a self in her or his own right. According to Bell, the Sun Chariot becomes a fast racing car such as a Trans-Am. The modern day family is the one-parent family that many youngsters have personally experienced. Although Bell's students have never ended the classical story with the death of the protagonist, the Trans-Am is nearly always destroyed. Most stories however end with a reconciliation of the family. This is a perfectly safe way for teenagers to resolve the created character's dilemma.

Suggested Teacher-Directed Strategies
1.   Students brainstorm for the prior knowledge they have acquired about myths.
2.   Choose a number of current popular movies today. Adventure stories such as *Rambo*, *Indiana Jones*, and *Star Wars* are well known by most students.

Identify the plot, character development, setting, theme, etc. Are there any common elements among the movies? Usually the skeletal plot of the monomyth will be elicited in some form here. Identify the story elements within a myth: plot, character development, setting, theme, etc. How do these elements compare with the parts of modern stories?

3.   Using a film such as *The Quest*, adapted from a story by Ray Bradbury, identify Campbell's pattern of the monomyth (Figure 2.1). This type of science-fiction film very vividly portrays the journey of personal growth at a metaphorical level. Other films recommended for this purpose are *Karate Kid I* and *II*, *The Emerald Forest*, *Windwalker*, and *Legend*. However almost any film will fit this pattern.

4.   Give the class the map of predictable life crises and possible life crises (Figure 2.4). Discuss how this map fits with the map of the journey of the hero/ine (Figure 2.1).

5.   Discuss the map of a spiral winding as a death/threshold/rebirth or an end/middle/beginning (Figure 2.5). Examples can be given of how a significant event in one's life can be viewed as comprising an end, a middle or passing through, and a new beginning. For instance, going on a holiday involves leaving home, entering the threshold of the vacation, and returning home again (a new beginning with a fresh viewpoint). To enter high school one must leave Grade 8 behind, and go through the trials and ordeals of finding one's way in high school, before finally, having internalized the high school culture, one can begin a new identity. Draw other examples from the class. Discuss the feelings and emotions that usually accompany such events.

6.   Using the graphic story map of the hero/ine's journey that has been depicted by Campbell (1973) in Figure 2.1, follow different variations of this journey through the prescribed steps of separation/initiation/return. The journeys of Odysseus, Perseus, Theseus, Buddha, Moses, or Luke Skywalker in *Star Wars* could be used.

7.   Using a skeletal plot, students can write a version of a modern day myth. This could be the hero/ine's adventure plot, or one from another story such as Phaeton.

8.   Have students construct a grid for a cross-classification chart and compare a mythic hero with a modern day hero (e.g., Odysseus and the American Western hero, Shane). Compare such qualities as physical strength, intelligence, personality traits, and loyalty. Write a paper on the differences between the two heroes. What do the differences say about our culture?

9.   In the ancient cultures the transition from one life stage to another was often marked by a ritual ceremony called a rite of passage. For example, a boy who was entering manhood would undergo a rite of passage ceremony to denote his new stature. Today there is little ritual to mark these rites of passage, although we still go through the same transitions. (A

contemporary example would be the Jewish bar mitzvah). Students could individually research a rite of passage from another culture. National Geographic magazines provide one good source, but there is a wide variety of popular literature examining this phenomena, including such books as *Songlines* (Chatwin, 1988). Describe what a rite of passage is, and show how the map of inner growth is or is not implicit in the rituals. Can students think of modern day rituals that could function as rites of passage? As a class, can they devise and carry out a modern day ritual?

Students could work in groups on a cross-classification chart which shows the cross-cultural similarities in rituals of rites of passage.

10. Students working in dyads choose two different myths. Each dyad chooses one of the following topics: demonstrating courage, showing determination, overcoming obstacles, taking risks, developing a sense of achievement, using inner resources, changing values, setting goals, pursuing ideals, helping others, or making a critical error. (Ideally there should not be more than two groups working on one topic.) Students are asked to review the myths carefully from the point of view of the chosen topic; develop a "big idea" or thesis statement based on their review; and support or refute their statement by using the two myths. A presentation of findings could be made to the class.

11. Students choose one of the characters in a myth with whom they can identify (or who in some way draws them), and write a monologue of this character's point of view during the event in the myth. This activity can be followed by a dramatic reading.

12. Have students write a dialogue between two characters in a myth that occurs several years after the myth ends. Two students can give a dramatic reading of this situation.

13. Role-play with a group to present a myth. A variation would be to role-play a modern version of the myth.

14. Choose a myth-inspired script designed for choral reading. It may be a student-prepared text (given the skeletal outline and specific directions for including a chorus, different groups could prepare different segments to combine for a class script), or a classical text such as *Antigone*. Discuss the meaning of the story and how it might be performed to best elicit the meaning through a choral reading. Practise the reading. Encourage students to suggest ways to improve the performance. Perform for another class.

15. Students artistically depict something that has meaning for them in the myth. This depiction could involve many different artistic approaches from making masks to representational art. Each student could explain to a small group the message behind her or his artwork.

16. The teacher reads the myth (having practised beforehand). The story is left at a crisis point. Students individually write a story about what happens

next. After each student's ending is shared, the teacher reads the original ending. A point of discussion could center on how closely the versions followed the monomyth.

17. Using the map of the journey of the hero/ine (Figure 2.1), examine ways in which the same pattern is found in nature. Students share different examples that they have researched.

18. Students can participate in the seasons by hands-on activities such as planting or harvesting. How does this fit with mythology?

19. Student activities could include designing a T-shirt to represent a favourite god, goddess, or hero/ine; creating a comic book based on a myth the students have read; writing an original poem inspired by a myth.

20. Students select a piece of music that complements the reading of a myth. Explain the choice. This music may actually be incorporated into any dramatic presentation.

21. Working in pairs or alone, students rewrite one myth into play format following the guidelines for play writing (setting, characterization, conflict, resolution, dialogue, stage directions). This play will be produced as a puppet show. Students are responsible for organizing and presenting the puppet show to the class. A copy of the play should be handed in.

22. Students read a picture-book version of a myth written for young children, create and illustrate a children's book based on a myth of their choice, then team up with a primary or junior class and read their storybook to a group of youngsters.

23. Have everyone sit in a circle (up to 20 can do this comfortably). With more students, divide the class, but keep an eye on both circles as this can become wild! One person begins telling the story of a chosen myth. The student to the orator's left goes to the middle of the circle and pantomimes as the story is told. The person speaking then passes the narration on to the next person on the left who picks up where she or he left off. The next person now gets up and acts. The alternating narrator and actor continue around the circle. The second time around the roles can be reversed. The story often deviates to some slight degree from the original plot which is part of the fun, but students should be familiar with the myth to keep it on track.

24. From a geographic perspective, have students write a travelogue based on a Greek or Roman myth which begins with a departure and ends with a return.

25. Participate in a cooking day where the typical modern cuisine of the cultures you are studying is the fare for the day. Groups can be responsible for the research, preparation, and presentation of different cuisine from other cultures. Costumes can enhance the event. Everyone samples all the dishes.

26. Students can participate in folk dances originating from the culture of the myth being studied.

27.   Have students research the Olympics in Ancient Greece. Hold a school
       sports day based on the early Grecian model.

Life Story and Mythology — Level 2

This level of study requires that students become familiar with connecting
narrative and mythology. First students need to understand certain concepts
involved in narrative. The telling of a life story or narrative gives unity and
coherence to the disparate parts of a person's life. It is rather like reading a book
with many chapters. The adventures in the chapters will be different, but there will
be a consistency or common thread throughout the book that establishes the
unique identity of the individual.

       Students also need to acquire an awareness of the temporal aspect of
narrative, that is, of how storytelling binds together the past, perceived present,
and anticipated future. The past has brought the individual to where she or he is
now; yet, the anticipated future also affects how one sees the present. The student
who has achieved success in the past and who anticipates the same in the future
will behave very differently in the present than the student who has experienced
failure and expects further failure.

       In addition, students need to be aware of the role of interpretation and
reconstruction in the telling of a life story. If they are undergoing a transition as
they reflect upon their story, their perception of the past will change. The events
will remain the same, but they will perceive them differently. They will also
perceive the future differently. It is a long and bumpy process. Eventually, after
many stops and starts, they will come to the realization that they have
reconstructed a new story. It is this new interpretation that allows them to see
the present differently and to behave in new ways.

       An individual's story can also be seen in the larger framework of the
universal mythology. When the interpretation of a story follows the road map for
the inner journey it can be viewed from a larger perspective. As described in Part
1 of this chapter, life crises such as the transitions into puberty, adulthood, middle
age, and old age can be viewed as predictable. One can be more fully prepared to
navigate these passages with greater awareness of their predictability. Significant
life events such as marriage, divorce, career changes, geographic changes, or
social changes that trigger growth can be seen as the chapters of a book or as
possible spirals on the path toward growth.

Suggested Teacher-Directed Strategies

1.   In small groups, students develop a spiral of significant life events that may
      be transformation periods for a young person travelling through the
      adolescent years. Examples may be a first love, unplanned pregnancy, or
      family breakup. Finally, develop a class model. Would they use a different
      symbol than the spiral? Why?

2. Students choose one life spiral of a major transition from the spiral the class developed. Construct a story around this spiral utilizing the map of the journey of the hero/ine (Figure 2.1). Compare stories. Use peer editing to verify the actual steps of the journey which are found in the story.

3. Have students choose a biography from a short story or historical personage or public hero (e.g., John Lennon). Using the predictable life transitions map of the inner journey (Figure 2.4), show how this person's story fits into the map. Examine one "chapter" of the story to see how it fits the end/middle/beginning model. If the character involved had been more aware of this map, how might this awareness have changed the actions of the character?

4. Students develop questions for an in-depth interview that will elicit the life story of someone (or perhaps one or two chapters). The questions should elicit feelings rather than strictly facts. Interview someone using the questions that were developed. Write a narrative of the life story of that person using the metaphor of the journey.

5. As a class develop the "Story of the Universe." Groups can be assigned different chapters. The story could explore the meaning of events in addition to the physical aspects of the universe known through science. The same elements of storytelling should be present as when telling a life story. As a class, review the complete story.

6. Students can be made aware of their own feelings about gender imagery for the god/dess. Ruether (1985) offers an exercise designed for such reflection. Imagine a god/dess in male gender terms. Sketch a symbol of yourself in relation to this god/dess. Write down what images or names come to mind. Now imagine a god/dess in female gender terms. Draw a symbol of yourself in relation to the female god/dess. Is there a difference? What is the difference? Compare the words that come to mind for god/dess as male or female. What kind of terms are these? What social roles do they suggest? Are there words that come to mind which are not based on gender roles? What are they? Draw a symbol of yourself in relation to the god/dess when using these non-gender-specific terms.

7. Have students use a short biographical story to explicate the principles of plot, character construction, setting, theme, etc. Using the same story look for the temporal aspects of biography. How has the past influenced the main character's present? How does the character anticipate the future? How does this anticipation of the future affect the perceived present? Suggest an alternative anticipated future. How would this change the present? The perception of the past?

8. Students reconstruct a biography or life story by changing the interpretation of some events in the past. Show how these changes might affect the interpretation of the anticipated future and perceived present.

9. Using a longer story (perhaps a novel or a historical personage), have

students look for the unity and coherence that integrates the disparate chapters in the book. What is the thread of unity in the life story?

The Life Story, Personal Mythology, and Mythology — Level 3

Students should now have a basic understanding of what telling a life story entails and of how the story can be connected to a larger, more universal framework. The work at this level becomes intensely personal and requires self-disclosure. The actual literary competence of a work should not be of prime importance at this point.

As the students reconstruct their own story they must risk vulnerability. It is extremely important, then, that the teacher has developed empathetic relationships and has proven herself or himself trustworthy. Students must be assured that the work they show to the teacher is confidential, and the class should be made aware of the confidentiality of material that is shared in class. Nevertheless, students should know that if they are not comfortable sharing some information (even in a small group learning situation) they can always pass without penalty. These ground rules seem to make students more comfortable and few will refuse to participate at some level.

Personal mythology is an integral part of any life story. The personal myth is a belief system or set of assumptions one holds about how the world operates. It is usually so deeply internalized that one is unaware of how this belief system guides and directs one's behaviour. Students need to be given a framework for understanding how a personal myth can develop and then influence one's life.

Feinstein and Krippner (1988) offer an example of how a personal mythology is constructed. A young boy who was born during the World War II era held John Wayne as his hero. At the core of his myth was a strong, rough, and confident image that guided his behaviour. The image of the ruggedly individualistic cowboy was internalized as the young boy constantly compared his life to that of John Wayne. Consciously or unconsciously he found ways to behave in tough, brave, or independent ways. He would constantly measure his behaviour against John Wayne's image. The ways in which he was positively reinforced for his behaviour by society, school, and family helped him determine that he was on the right course. His mythology evolved according to what happened to him in his life. It was only when he entered middle age that he discovered that this personal mythology was not working anymore. In living this myth, he was not able to express the sensitive side of himself that he was now discovering. This conflict indicated that a new personal mythology was emerging.

The personal myth tends to be self-fulfilling. For example, if one decided early in life that the world was an unloving place, the individual may unconsciously act in ways that allow her or him to avoid intimate contact. A teenager who has trouble with authority figures may find herself or himself repeatedly having difficulty with this type of figure through all the life stages.

An individual's personal myth can change through either dramatic crisis or gradual evolution. How do people know when a myth needs to change? A myth is not working when one's behaviour does not match one's beliefs. When experience does not match personal myths, one has two choices: alter perceptions of experience, or change one's myth. The transitional period between one life passage and another represents a crisis in identity.

When one begins to experience conflict, has difficulty making decisions, acts in ways that do not fit one's concept of self, or perhaps even becomes ill, it can be a signal that a new personal mythology is emerging (Feinstein & Krippner, 1988). These changes may indicate a stage of transition and that a new constellation of beliefs, values, assumptions, and behaviours is emerging.

Adolescents, by the very nature of their changing bodies, are in such a period of transition. They must shift their identity from one way of being to another. They are at a point where they have the cognitive structure to perform the formal operations necessary to organize their personal narrative. They can construct their life story so that their growth and development is congruent with their new emerging personal mythology.

The crises in a young person's life are accompanied by a breakdown in personal mythology. This is the time to let go of an outdated myth and allow a new myth to emerge. Usually it is a synthesis of the old and the emerging myth that an individual eventually adopts as the guiding model for behaviour. Typically, this emergence of a new myth from the synthesis of the old and the new are outside the individual's awareness. However, if young people can become aware of this process at a conscious level, they have a greater chance of resolving the personal mythology conflicts satisfactorily.

At this point, the teacher may differentiate between a life story, personal mythology, and universal mythology. Everyone has a life story through which there is a thread of unity and coherence. The life story can be embedded in the pattern of universal mythology in that everyone must undergo the hero/ine's adventure when navigating the predictable life crises. At the same time, we are guided by a personal mythology which changes as we grow, develop, and navigate these passages of life. This personal mythology is always present in the life story and can also be linked to a larger framework, the monomyth of the inner journey. All mythology is culture-bound, yet it still has a universal structure. Similarly, personal mythology is individual-bound, yet still fits into the universal pattern of the inner journey.

The life story continues, chapter upon chapter, spiral upon spiral. Our personal mythologies change as we move from one spiral to the next. Yet, the archetypal structure of universal mythology remains the same. It tells us the same message again and again. It is this message that can be integrated into the life stories and personal mythologies of young people to help them make sense and meaning out of their lives. Mythology tells us that if we are to develop and grow, we must continually experience a cycle taking us from death to rebirth. As we make our way through the journey of life, we will experience this phenomena as an ending, middle, beginning (Foster & Little, 1988). As was discussed earlier, the ending signifies the death of at least a part of our current personal mythology; the middle represents the ordeals and trials that we will encounter in the process of letting go of the old and embracing the new. Finally, the beginning signifies the birth of a new way of valuing, believing, and behaving. This is a new way of being, a new story, and a new personal mythology.

The wisdom gleaned in mythology tells us to celebrate these passages of transition, these periods of change and growth. We are urged to accept the challenge of letting go of the old, knowing that it will involve suffering and pain. We are told to get on with our lives, to become unstuck. And finally, most importantly, we are cautioned to look into our heart and listen to our own inner voice to know intuitively what our next step should be.

The strategies offered are designed to facilitate awareness of the following:

+ Constructing one's life story from the perspective of the spiralling map of inner growth offered by mythology.
+ Identifying a transitional point. This transition is often evidenced by the experience of personal conflict, unfamiliar fears, difficulties making a decision, and confusion.
+ Recognizing and examining the current personal myth. This examination involves looking at the history and background of the individual. It is also helpful to understand how this myth has been useful in the past.
+ Identifying and evaluating the values, beliefs, and behaviours that accompany the emerging myth.
+ Synthesizing the old personal myth and the emerging myth so that one has a realistic scenario of the future that will act as a guiding mythology.
+ Listening to one's inner voice as a guide to the right next step in one's journey of personal growth. Our inner voice speaks the same archetypal language as that of the mythology. Mythology, then, offers us a powerful tool with which to authenticate our own inner wisdom.

Suggested Teacher-Directed Strategies

1. The teacher gives the following instructions: Think of your life story as if it were being plotted on a spiral. Each winding marks periods of growth and development. At the end of each winding you are a different person than you were at the beginning. To help you think of this process, recall the significant events in your life. Personal growth and development require a cycle of birth, death, and rebirth, or an ending, middle, and beginning.

Reinterpret your story through this model. Does it fit? Why or why not? Your spiral may not look the same as the one suggested in this chapter. How would you draw your spiral?

2. The teacher gives the following instructions: Think of your life as a series of chapters in a book. In some ways you are the same person from the beginning to the end. Yet, in other ways you have grown and changed. Divide those growth periods into chapters (these probably parallel the spiral windings). Name each chapter. Give a short plot summary for each chapter.

3. An important part of the personal narrative is one's environmental autobiography. How far can you go back in time? How does the natural world speak to you? How did you and your family communicate with the environment? How would you like your native place to fit into the Great Story of the Universe? To set the scene for this exercise the teacher can take the students through a visualization exercise which covers the beginning of time to the present. This is an adaptation of a Thomas Berry (1990) exercise.

4. In order to elicit the family history, students can be instructed in the following exercise: You belong to a social group or culture which has rules, customs, traditions, and habitual ways of acting. For example, what spoken or unspoken commandments best summarize the rules of your family? These become a large part of your assumptions about the world. Students understand how these assumptions operate if you use the analogy of a message being like an old tape which automatically plays on the tape recorder of your brain when you get into certain situations. Think about what family mythology you grew up with. What were the real messages or old tapes you got about your intelligence, your appearance, love, marriage, education, having children, divorce, sex, money, career, women, men (e.g., big boys do not cry; education is very important)? Write these down. Sometimes these assumptions are difficult to discover. What did people say? What did people do? Now write down how these views affect you in your life today.

5. Students identify personal hero/ines. What qualities of the archetypal hero/ine are similar to the personal hero/ine?

6. Develop an ideal scenario of the future. The teacher asks the students to relax and shut their eyes. She or he tells the students that they are going on a time machine journey into the future where they will be able to see their ideal future. She or he instructs them to get into the time machine that takes them into the future. Once at their destination students look at their ideal life from the point of view of professional, social, and family interests, leisure time, etc. Then the teacher brings them back in the time machine to their desks. The students write about their ideal future as if they were writing a page in their journals two years from now. Evaluate how

grounded in reality the vision is. Is the vision possible? Realistic? Do they like the values that underlie their choices?

7. The following exercise is designed to help students become unstuck and move on to what's next. The teacher asks the students if they can remember a time in their lives when they kept repeating a negative pattern over and over. Some examples might be staying in a negative relationship, continually putting oneself down, not taking that positive risk, or abusing alcohol or drugs. Write a story about the past events of your life story that got you to that stuck place. What was the anticipated future here? How did you reconstruct the story to get unstuck? Think of an area where you are stuck today. How can you reconstruct the story to get unstuck? (What have we learned from mythology that might help? How does your ideal future fit in here?)

8. One of the themes of mythology is that of the hero/ine being critically wounded. The wound, although it causes severe pain, has many positive side effects and leads to personal growth. The wound may be physical, such as an illness or act of violation, or may result from losses, such as of a significant relationship or a job. It may come from a critical error that the hero/ine has made. The wounding becomes transformational when we are willing to release our old story and allow a new story to emerge. When we fail to do this the old story tends to repeat itself over and over again. Houston (1987) suggests that these types of woundings mark the core of all great western myths: Adam's rib, Achilles' heel, Odin's eye, Orpheus's decapitation, Prometheus's liver, Zeus's split head, Persephone's rape, Oedipus's blinding. To capture this process, students can draw on a sheet of paper something to represent a critical error or wounding from the past. Then they draw images that represent short- and long-term results of that event. Have students share their drawings with a partner. The teacher could ask: Can you see this experience from a mythological perspective? Look at other mythological themes from this viewpoint. How has betrayal or personal loss helped you to grow? This approach is an adaptation of a Jean Houston (1987) exercise.

9. Students present their life stories from the perspective of the mythical god or goddess of their choice to two other gods or goddesses (also playing a role). The speaker talks for about five minutes about the present dilemma of her or his life. For example a young woman might say: "Look at Susan. She is really stuck. She wants so much to please her parents and do what they want her to do. But she also feels that she should go away to school. At the same time she doesn't want to leave her boyfriend behind and he is pressuring her to stay." At the end of five minutes, the other two goddesses or gods may ask questions. Everyone should remember to stay in her or his mythological role.

    After this part of the activity has been completed, each goddess or god should have one minute to say what it is that the "mere mortal" really wants. "What Susan really wants is the courage to get up and go on." This exercise allows students to see themselves from a distanced and larger perspective. This is an adaptation of a Jean Houston (1987) exercise.

10. Students make a list of 10 things that make them deeply happy. (The 10 things must not cost money!) How often do they do those things? If they do not do them often, why not?

11. The teacher reads a myth or story. Students choose one character with whom they identify. They shut their eyes and allow an image to emerge. Work with that image as a personal metaphor. How does it fit with your life? Is there a message to be learned from it? Become the image and talk with it. What message does it have for you? Write down what you have learned.

12. Visualization can be achieved by playing music and encouraging students to let their imaginations go. The teacher can start off the exercise with an image, for example: "You are standing by the edge of a river watching the water drift by. It looks so inviting that you decide that you will float down the river too. You find yourself floating down the river. You feel the sun rest warmly on your body and head. You feel a breeze brush over your body. On either side of the river you notice the lush vegetation. You feel relaxed and peaceful as you float down the river...."

The teacher then allows the students to go into their own fantasy worlds as the music plays for about five minutes. Near the end of the five minutes the teacher can gently remind students that they will be coming back to the classroom in their own time. As they come back to the present situation, students are asked to open their eyes slowly and stretch. Then they can tell their experience to others and/or write a story of the experience.

Some music selections suggested by Jean Houston (1987) are "Equinox," Jean Michael Jarre, Polydor PD-1675; "Oxygene," Jean Michael Jarre, Polydor 2933-207; "Heaven and Hell," Vangelis Papathanassiou, RCA LPL1-5110; "Chariots of Fire" (especially Eric's theme), Polygram Records Kosmos; "Tomita," RCA ARL1-2616; "Hooked on Classics," RCA AYK I5022; "Love at the Greek," Neil Diamond, Columbia X1198; "Violin Concerto in D" (especially the first movement), Tchaikovsky, Angel-EM1 4XSS-32807.

The result for most students will be a visualization. This fantasy often corresponds with the pattern in the archetypal journey. Regardless of the content of an individual's visualization, the student can be asked to write a story based on this experience. Generally some very imaginative pieces of work will be elicited. Once a story has been written, the students can be asked how the story they have created relates to their own present life. The question can be very thought-provoking, and the teacher and perhaps class members, can help with the discussion, if the student chooses to share her or his work. Finally, students can be asked if the story relates to the journey of the hero/ine or archetypes in any way.

Learning to Live Mythically — Level 4

At this level, the student is actually learning to behave in ways that are in accordance with a highly developed personal myth congruent with universal mythology. This behaviour requires commitment to a vision that sees beyond oneself. The larger perspective is available to us through the symbols and metaphors of mythology. It is also accessible through reflection, meditation, and listening to the inner voice.

Living according to a story larger than one's own, individuals tend to see the world in different ways. As Joseph Campbell (1988) suggests, the new mythology has to be a mythology of the planet, a mythology that stresses the interconnections among all people and the interdependence of all things. A more universal perspective leads people to be more sensitive and compassionate toward their planet and their fellow travellers. As one proceeds along the inner path, suffering as well as joy, love, and compassion are experienced. One is fully alive and takes full responsibility for oneself.

Humans tend to resist change. It is more comfortable to stay with the known. Yet the map of the inner journey urges one onward, stepping again and again into the unknown with only the inner voice and mythology as a guide. Everyone needs techniques and encouragement to stay on track. The process of transformation requires hard, dedicated perseverance.

The teacher is really a guide at this level. The student becomes the expert concerning her or his own journey.

Suggested Teacher-Directed Strategies

1.   Quiet Time: Build a meditation time into class. Students learn to really appreciate this time for reflection and for being able to listen to their own still small voice. (The teacher can begin by having reluctant students put their heads down on their desks.) It is helpful to play some classical music.
2.   Journal Writing: Students keep a regular log where they reflect on their goals and make a commitment to acting in ways to actualize those goals. The journal also serves as a place for students to reflect on their actions. This reflection should be done through the lenses of the map of the inner journey. These journals can be regularly handed in to the teacher who can begin to engage in a powerful dialogue with the student through written correspondence. If the student does not wish to have a journal entry read, she or he can fold the page over.
3.   Students can rehearse desired actions or experience them through visualization. Psychosynthesis offers exercises which "condition" the mind to experience the transpersonal. Psychosynthesis is an approach to personal

growth that includes not only the actualization of human potentialities, but also the realization of the Self (Ferrucci, 1982). Psychosynthesis is concerned with the harmonious and well-balanced development of the mental, physical, and spiritual aspects of the human body. Techniques offered in psychosynthesis include the Higher Self which is unaffected by conscious experiences. The techniques can elicit transformation and are particularly effective in the classroom setting.

What We May Be by Piero Ferrucci (1982) offers rich experiential exercises. Of particular interest are exercises such as "The Rose" or "The Butterfly" which condition the mind to experience the transpersonal. These exercises convey the sense of the unfolding of the psyche and at the same time facilitate it. Diana Whitmore's (1986) *Psychosynthesis in Education* is an excellent book offering practical exercises. Written specifically for teachers working with adolescents, the book offers many invaluable strategies that move from identity struggles to becoming more than one thinks is possible.

4.   The Wise Person Visualization: This visualization helps students gain access to their inner voice when actively confronting a problem. Students should be told to reflect on a serious dilemma before starting this exercise. Students close their eyes and the teacher has them perform a relaxation sequence. The following instructions can be read: "You find yourself in a beautiful meadow on a warm spring day. You feel the warmth of the sun on you body, the gentle breeze on your skin. You smell the freshness of the meadow and you feel relaxed and peaceful. In the distance there is a mountain. You find yourself quickly following the path through the meadow until you are at the base of the mountain. Now you climb up the mountain. It is an easy climb. From the top of the mountain you can look around at the world below you.

"You sense the presence of a friendly being on this mountain top, and suddenly you know you are in the company of a wise person. You look carefully into the accepting face of the wise person and you introduce yourself. You realize you can ask this person about anything that is either troubling you or of which you are uncertain. You look into the kindly eyes of the wise person and explain your situation. Then you listen carefully to the words of your companion, knowing that you will be given the solution or part of the solution to your problem. Allow two or three minutes of silent time for this insight to be revealed.

"Now you have heard the wisdom of your wise person and you will take it back to the world to reflect upon it. You may have been surprised by the words you have heard, but you know that you have heard things that are true for you at some level. You thank your wise person and arrange a way in which you may meet again. Then you say goodbye.

"You travel quietly down the mountain path... and back through the meadow until you are at the place where you started. Now very gently, and on your own time, you come back to the here and now."

5.   Students can use their journals for personal reflections. The following instructions can trigger reflections: Everyone has a personal mythology that guides her or his behaviour. The mythology is a constellation of beliefs, values, and images that are organized around a core theme. In reviewing your life story, decide how your own personal mythology might read. Consider your own life now. Where are you? Where are you going? How must you behave to get there? Starting from these questions, describe how you could best navigate the current journey. Write this account in the third person with you, the narrator, as the "wise person" who knows what is best for your character.

6.   Use of Affirmations: Students use affirmations to reinforce the positive things about themselves that they are developing.

  "I, Tim, am a caring loving person."
  "I, Roberta, am lovoable."
  "I, Tom, am a worthy person."

7.   Visualization of the Ideal Self: Students can be taught to visualize themselves acting in positive ways that reinforce their emerging personal mythology. The sequence involves a relaxation followed by a visualization in which the individual imagines herself or himself acting in ideal ways. The "ideal model" (Ferrucci, 1982) offers one version of the exercise and focuses on visualizing qualities such as love, strength, joy, and understanding. According to Ferrucci, the ideal model technique is based on the freedom of the individual to influence her or his own destiny. The important point is to be certain that the chosen goal is in line with one's purpose in life. This powerful exercise can be used in both constructive and destructive ways. By focusing on the map of the inner journey, the student can become aware of her or his own existing blueprint and utilize the exercise in positive ways.

SUMMARY

This chapter has offered a conceptual framework for teachers to bring mythology into the classroom in an interdisciplinary fashion. The personal narrative can be embedded in a larger story as a guide through transformation. Since we are living on a planet which is rapidly becoming a global community, all people increasingly need a perspective for living which recognizes the interconnections among all things. Mythology can help clarify these connections. Although we are living in an age of unprecedented change, all people across cultures from the beginning of humanity have experienced change in much the same way. We are not so different from each other or our ancestors in that we need to learn to successfully negotiate change in order to survive. Looking to the wisdom passed down through mythology, we find a history of negotiating change. Mythology, then, offers an invaluable tool for living fully today.

REFERENCES

Bell, W. (1983). Mythology and maturation. In M. Fleming (Ed.), *Arizona English Bulletin*. Arizona: ED274 993.

Berry, T. (1988). *The dream of earth.* San Francisco: Sierra Club Books.

Berry, T. (1990, March 17). The universe story: The role of the human in the story. Seminar held by the Canadian Institute of Cultural Affairs at The Ontario Institute for Studies in Education, Toronto.

Blackmer, J. (1989). *Acrobats of the gods: Dance and transformation.* Toronto: Inner City Books.

Bolen, J. (1984). *Goddesses in everywoman: A new psychology of women.* New York: Harper & Row.

Bolen, J. (1989). *Gods in everyman.* San Francisco: Harper & Row.

Campbell, J. (1973). *The hero with a thousand faces.* New York: Meridan Books.

Campbell, J. (1988). *The power of myth.* Toronto: Doubleday.

Chatwin, B. (1988). *Songlines.* New York: Penguin.

Clark, E. (1989). Environmental education as an integrative study. *Holistic Education Review*, 2(3), 54-62.

Cohen, M. J. (1988). *How nature works: Regenerating kinship with planet earth.* Toronto: Fitzhenry & Whiteside.

Eisler, R. T. (1987). *The chalice and the blade: Our history, our future.* San Francisco: Harper & Row.

Erodes, R., & Ortiz, A. (1984). *American Indian myths and legends.* New York: Pantheon Books.

Feinstein, D., & Krippner, S. (1988). *Personal mythology: The psychology of your evolving self.* Los Angeles: Jeremy P. Tarcher.

Ferrucci, P. (1982). *What we may be: Techniques for psychological and spiritual growth.* Los Angeles: Jeremy P. Tarcher.

Foster, S., & Little, M. (1988). The fasting quest as a modern rite of passage. *Holistic Education Review, 1*(3), 30-35.

Gimbutas, M. A. (1982). *Goddesses and gods of old Europe, 6500-3500 BC: Myths and cult images.* London: Tames and Hudson.

Houston, J. (1987). *The search for the beloved: Journeys in sacred psychology.* Los Angeles: Jeremy P. Tarcher.

Jung, C. (1964). *Man and his symbols.* New York: Doubleday.

Knappert, J. (1986). *Kings, gods and spirits from African mythology.* Toronto: Douglas & McIntyre.

Maddern, E. (1990). What fifteen year olds need. *Green Teacher, 18,* 12-16.

Martin, H. (1988). Running wolf: Vision quest and the inner life of the middle school student. *Holistic Education Review, 1*(3), 36-39.

McAdams, D. (1985). *Power, intimacy and the life story: Personological inquiries into identity.* Homewood, IL: Dorsey Press.

Miller, R. (1988). The quest for vision: An interview with Joseph Jastrab. *Holistic Education Review, 1*(3), 40-43.

Noble, K. (1990). The female hero: A quest for healing and wholeness. *Women and Therapy, 9*(4), 3-18.

Olds, L. E. (1981). *Fully human: How everyone can integrate the benefits of masculine and feminine sex roles.* Englewood Cliffs, NJ: Prentice-Hall.

Pearson, C. (1986). *The hero within: Six archetypes we live by.* San Francisco: Harper & Row.

Purce, J. (1980). *The mystic spiral.* London: Thames and Hudson.

Ruether, R. (1986). *Womanguides: Readings toward a feminist theology.* Boston: Beacon Press.

Sarbin, T. (1986). *Narrative psychology: The storied nature of human conduct.* New York: Praeger.

Weigle, M. (1982). *Spiders & spinsters: Women & mythology.* Albuquerque: University of New Mexico Press.

Wells, G. (1988). Stories are for understanding. In *Growing with Books. Book I: Literature and education* (pp. 8-22). Toronto: Ontario Ministry of Education.

White, T. (1950). *The golden treasury of myths and legends.* New York: Golden Press.

Whitmore, D. (1986). *Psychosynthesis in education: A guide to the joy of learning.* Rochester, VT: Destiny Books.

Woodman, M. (1982). *Addiction to perfection.* Toronto: Inner City Books.

CHAPTER 3

HUMAN PROCESSES: PROBLEM SOLVING

The inability of the real world to be compartmentalized means that any kind of problem-solving activity requires an interest in the general system that underlies the problem and cannot be confined to any one discipline....

The search for the unity of human knowledge comes from the faith, perhaps a little blind, in the fundamental unity of the real world and its interconnectedness. (Boulding, 1981, p. 28, 29)

As noted in the first chapter, human processes involve the ways that people make sense of their experience and include such things as a sense of wonder, an urge to discover, and a need to unravel puzzles or problems. Human processes involve, then, the way we interact with the world. It is possible to relate to the world within the framework of the three positions (transmission, transaction, and transformation). At the transmission level there can be a tendency to see the world as an object to be manipulated, or in terms of what Martin Buber (1947) called the "I-it" relationship. At this level we are more interested in trying to control the world than in discovering or understanding it.

At the transaction level we tend to relate to the world through our mental processes. Cognitive psychologists claim that our thinking structures, or schemata, provide the principal means for "framing" our experiences and interactions with our world.

At the transformation level we relate to the world through our Being, or Emerson's (see p. 3) "big fellow," which allows us to see the world as interdependent and interconnected. Human processes at this level are characterized by a sense of discovery and wonder.

In this chapter we look at one problem-solving strategy that can facilitate human processes. A *strategy* is viewed here as a structured approach that allows us to work with human processes in a classroom setting. Specifically, we look at transactional and transformational approaches to problem solving.

The curriculum in most schools in Canada is designed to foster the development and well-being of the learner and, at the same time, to prepare students for the labour market. In Ontario, the Ministry of Education described in a document entitled *Issues and Directions* (June 1980) an "ideal picture" of the learner. The learner was described as "a self-motivated, self-directed problem-solver, aware of both the processes and uses of learning and deriving a sense of self-worth and confidence from a variety of accomplishments" (p. 3). The statement goes on to describe the ideal learner as "a methodical thinker who is capable of inquiry, analysis, synthesis, and evaluation, as well as a perceptive discoverer" (pp. 2-3). This theme is reiterated as one of the 13 goals of education for the Province of Ontario.

While the call for holism seemed to originate in part from general dissatisfaction with curricula that deal almost exclusively with the cognitive domain, one would be remiss to assume that the holistic curriculum does not encompass problem-solving and inquiry skills. Clearly, problem solving and inquiry represent a significant part of students' learning within the holistic curriculum. Our challenge is not only for those who deal exclusively with cognitive goals and objectives; we also regard an overemphasis on the affective curriculum as an inappropriate imbalance in the holistic intention.

In this chapter, then, we shift our attention from developing a personal mythology to problem-solving and inquiry skills instruction. That lessons in problem solving and inquiry promote the holistic curriculum is obvious. What is not so apparent is the particular ways in which this curricular intention is realized. In our view, there are three aspects of holism that can be addressed by problem solving and instruction. Moreover, each of these areas of focus can be used to measure how well a lesson or unit in problem solving facilitates holistic learning.

(i) *Interdisciplinary Linkage.* A key consideration in holism is the concept "connectedness." In the ideal holistic curriculum, the artificial barriers between disciplines would vanish. Students would not think of Keyboarding as separate from Environmental Studies, and of Mathematics as unconnected to History. Rather, the interdisciplinary linkages are an inherent aspect of learning. Subject area specialization can sometimes atomize or fracture learning. In the holistic curriculum, the logical, practical, and indeed the aesthetic connectedness of seemingly diverse learning content is featured.

(ii) *Expansion of Goals and the Curriculum.* Although some educators and the general public appear to share rather traditional notions about what schools should "teach" and what students should "learn," the curriculum has greatly expanded in the last two decades. In many schools students learn deep relaxation techniques, they routinely experience visualization exercises, and they are encouraged to listen to the "creative voice within." The holistic curriculum broadens traditional learning to include all aspects of one's being — whether cognitive, affective, physical, spiritual, or aesthetic — and thereby extends the curriculum itself.

(iii) *The Active Learner*. Since one major goal of education is to help the learner become all she or he is capable of becoming, the extent to which the learner participates in and assumes responsibility for the learning becomes a significant consideration. In our view the traditional transmission orientation of instruction frequently failed to involve the learner. The transactional climate, wherein the teacher and learner are viewed as learning partners, represents a major shift toward the desired direction. The ultimate level of learner involvement would be characterized by self-initiated, self-directed and self-monitored learning. This level, from our perspective, culminates in the transformational orientation.

In this chapter we describe both transactional (the Ontario Institute for Studies in Education Field Services group model) and transformational (the Creative Problem Solving and the Wallas models) approaches to problem solving. The approaches are not presented fully; rather, the salient features of the approaches will be our initial focus, followed by an analysis of their contribution to the holistic curriculum, and practical exercises which have transdisciplinary applicability throughout the intermediate and senior divisions.

In the interest of simplicity and practicality, we use the terms "inquiry" and "problem solving" synonymously. Thinking skills represent individual mental operations required as part of the problem-solving process; decision making is viewed as one type of problem solving (as is comparative analysis or logical analysis, and so forth).

Our selection of the models and approaches to problem solving is some-what arbitrary, given the plethora of approaches from which to choose. Paul Chance (1986), provides a detailed analysis of programs that teach "thinking in the classroom." Nickerson, Perkins, and Smith (1985), and Segal, Chipman, and Glaser (1985) also review the teaching of thinking skills. The latter two texts, however, present a more scholarly analysis than the former of both the issues and programs associated with thinking skills.

We have chosen to highlight aspects of the holistic curriculum by selecting a few particular approaches to problem solving. Within these approaches, we isolate particular features that represent either transactional or transformational intentions, leaving a comprehensive presentation of individual approaches to further reading.

THE ONTARIO GROUP

For more than 20 years, Professor Floyd Robinson of the Ontario Institute for Studies in Education (OISE) has led various teams of academics and professionals in the pursuit of curriculum models and strategies to improve children's thinking processes. To date, his OISE Field Services (OFS) group has generated a compendium of curriculum products that span grades and disciplines. Foremost among their accomplishments are: an innovative graduate program to instruct educators in the use of their curriculum systems; a comprehensive set of curriculum development strategies to "program" complex educational objectives; an interdisciplinary inquiry skills list (IDSL); a topic development system to link the teaching of content to students' thought processes; and a set of frameworks (externalized schemata) for developing students' skills across a diverse range of inquiry or problem-solving contexts.

The OFS group has produced an extensive set of resource documents that use framework-based problem-solving models. Among these are contributions by C. Bennett, J. R. B. Cassie, D. Gruber, F. Maynes, N. Maynes, L. Popp, F. G. Robinson, J. Ross, and F. White (OFS group documents are available from Field Centres of the Ontario Institute for Studies in Education, see Appendix A for addresses). Recent work involves a jointly developed model for the intentional holistic learner. This model provides a base so that the critical components of various problem-solving models can be synthesized.

THE SEARCH FOR AN INTERDISCIPLINARY PROBLEM-SOLVING MODEL

In the late 1960s, when the Ontario Ministry of Education guidelines started to feature the idea of problem solving, educators began to look for a general problem-solving model that would suit the needs of all the school disciplines. Many school systems made full use of the so-called researching model which had as its main steps:

1. State the problem to be solved in the form of a question.
2. Gather information.
3. Organize the information.
4. Draw conclusions from the organized information.
6. Communicate the findings (written or oral).

Another model, derived from Dewey's (1933) famous book, *How We Think*, became very popular when it appeared in an Ontario Ministry of Education resource document, *Research Study Skills* (1979). This model is reprinted on page 69 (Figure 3.1).

The adoption and use of the above model (and its numerous facsimiles), particularly in the junior and intermediate divisions, met with both success and failure. When the model was applied to "real life" decisions, it was welcomed as

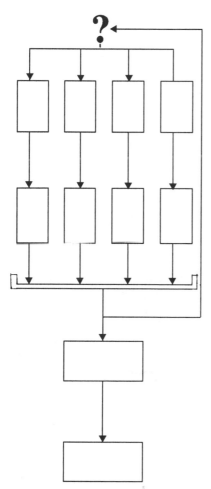

Initial experience:
Exploratory activities are introduced

Question:
The student poses a suitable question
around which the study will develop.

Alternatives:
The student suggests a range of reasonable
alternatives to answer the question.
(Additional alternatives may arise in the
subsequent data-collection stage.)

Data:
The student collects information on each
alternative.

Synthesis:
The student arrives at a conclusion by
deciding, on the basis of the accumulated
information, which of the alternatives
give(s) the best answer to the question.

Assessing the Conclusion:
The student ascertains whether the
conclusion adequately answers the original
question.

Expressing the Conclusion:
The student organizes a clear expression
and presentation of the conclusion.

Evaluation:
The student assesses the appropriateness
of the conclusion and its expression in the
light of the original question.

Figure 3.1

Note. From *Research Study Skills* (Figure 5), 1979, Toronto: Ontario Ministry of
Education. Copyright 1979 by the Queen's Printer for Ontario. Reprinted with
permission from the Queen's Printer for Ontario.

a suitable set of steps leading from a decision question (for example, "What is the best way to get to Toronto from location X?") to a logical response. However, the model required considerable adaptation and refinement for use in subject disciplines. Various members of the OFS group made creative adjustments to the general model, seeking to increase its applicability to discipline-specific contexts.

By 1975, numerous attempts had been made to apply inquiry skills to the subject disciplines, notably in science, mathematics, geography, history, and guidance. Teachers in different disciplines began to compare their versions of the problem-solving model, placing particular emphasis on the visual representations (frameworks) that were implicit or explicit in them. What eventually emerged was a comprehensive set of steps that would subsume all the individual models. The OFS group now call this their Interdisciplinary Inquiry Skills List (IDSL). Below is the Ross and Maynes (1982) version of the IDSL, although it should be noted that refinements which have not yet been published have since been made to the list.

Defining the problem. The first step involves "establishing a focus for the inquiry and defining the elements of the problem to be solved, or identifying the question to be answered." The skill the student develops in this step is the ability to narrow her or his focus of concern to a definable problem.

Establishing a framework for the inquiry. The student forms a mental image of the problem and its solution. The goal here is for the student to develop an overall conception of the problem and how the various elements involved relate to one another. The student begins by developing an internal image of the problem, and then conveys the problem in a visible form, as a table, graph, or diagram for example. Ross and Maynes claim that this is the most important skill in problem solving and that the "failure to provide assistance to students in developing competence in this skill is the major factor impeding growth in problem-solving performance."

Determining sources of data. The student identifies resources (e.g., books, maps) that can help solve the problem.

Obtaining data at source. The student assesses the selected data with regard to their relevance, accuracy, and quantity.

Putting data into a framework. The student organizes the relevant data. For example, the skill may involve putting the data into a table or graph.

Reducing data to summary form. In this step the student performs simple calculations, such as averaging or computing percentages, in order to interpret the data within the framework.

Observing relationships among the data. The student looks for trends in the data. This skill may involve statistically establishing or refuting a relationship between two or more variables.

Interpreting data. The student accurately records the relationships observed in the preceding step.

Extrapolating the interpretation. At this point the student generalizes and applies to different contexts the conclusions she or he draws. This skill involves making predictions about new situations.

Communicating an inquiry. The student reports the results of the problem-solving exercise. This reporting is the final product of problem solving.

This procedure is featured in the geography (1988) and history (1986) guidelines produced by the Ontario Ministry of Education. The student using these inquiry skills in both disciplines would gain a sense of how these two disciplines can be connected through these skills. The list can also be applied to literature appreciation (Maynes & Ross, 1985) and to writing. Table 3.1 shows how the IDSL has been applied to four Ontario Secondary Schools: Intermediate Senior (OS:IS) guidelines. Observation of Table 3.1 will show that while not every guideline covers all the IDSL skills, there is no IDSL skill that is not present in at least one of the four guidelines. Secondly, disciplines tend to make use of a discipline-specific language. For example, the IDSL skill, "communicate the inquiry and its results," is written in the history guideline as, "communicate: express information and ideas and describe the process involved"; in the science guideline it is, "present results in a clear and concise manner."

Therefore, with minor variations in the wording of guideline statements, they can be aligned with the IDSL terms. The major advantage here, according to the OFS group, is that the IDSL can be used as a comprehensive skills organizer regardless of the discipline being engaged. From this common base, educators can align curricular emphases to maximize students' facility with the broad range of inquiry skills. While the order of skills listed indicates the overall flow of mental activity, the OFS group does not advocate a rigid linear progression. There can be large "loops"; somewhere along the route, the inquirer may decide that the framework was too small, or that the question was incorrect, and will loop back to rethink this segment of the inquiry (hopefully at a new level). Moreover, it is possible to start at some point other than the "focus": it is quite common, for example, for an interesting observation of a piece of data to stimulate a question that leads to subsequent inquiry.

Example of Interdisciplinary Skills in Intermediate Guidelines

IDSL 1987	HISTORY 1986	GEO-GRAPHY 1988	SCIENCE 1987	FAMILY STUDIES 1987
Surface feelings and associated thoughts about the topic				Initial experience of exploratory activities
Establish a focus for the inquiry.	Focus: limit, direct or define a problem or issue.	Focus: limit, direct or define a topic, problem, or issue.	Formulate a working hypothesis.	Formulate inquiry question which clarifies and focuses on the essential issue.
Establish a framework for the inquiry.	Organize: select or develop a visual representation chart or organizer for the focus.	Organize: select or develop a visual representation chart or organizer for the focus.	Design appropriate procedures for performing experiments.	Develop a set of alternative solutions.
Locate sources of information.	Locate: identify, find, and use reliable, relevant sources of information.	Locate: identify, find, and use reliable, relevant sources of information.	Select appropriate measuring instruments.	Locate desired information.
Obtain the information at the source.	Locate: identify, find and use reliable, relevant sources of information.	Locate: identify, find and use reliable, relevant sources of information.	Observe objects and phenomena.	Collect information.
Assess the adequacy of the information.	Determine the reliability of sources of information.	Use reliable information.	Estimate measure-ments and recognize limits of accuracy.	Interpret the data.
Record information on the framework.	Record: record information and relate to appropriate parts of organizer.	Record: put the information into the framework.	Process experimental data.	

Summarize the information.	Summarize the information.	Summarize the information.	Present data in the form of functional relationships.	Assess critically the value of the data.
Determine relationships in the summary data.	Evaluate/ Assess: determine validity, appropriateness, significance and accuracy.	Evaluate/ Assess: determine validity, appropriateness, significance and accuracy.		Successively eliminate alternatives as negative data emerges.
Interpret the relationships.	Synthesize/ Conclude: observe relationships in and draw conclusions from information.	Synthesize/ Conclude: make connections within and draw conclusions from information.	Interpret experimental data and observations.	State the conclusion.
Evaluate the process and product of the inquiry.	Re-examine appropriateness of focus and organizer.	Re-examine appropriateness of focus and organizer.	Evaluate hypothesis under test in light of data obtained.	Ascertain whether conclusion adequately answers the original question.
Modify the process where required.	Adjust focus and organize as necessary.	Adjust focus and organizer.		Review and make improvements in the procedure.
Extrapolate the process and product beyond the inquiry.	Apply: predict, generalize, compare, and decide base on conclusions.	Apply: predict, generalize.	Extrapolate: formulate generalization.	Apply the conclusion to other contexts.
Communicate the inquiry and its results.	Communicate: express information and ideas and describe the process involved.	Communicate: express information, ideas, and process involved.	Present results in a clear and concise manner.	Express the conclusion.

Table 3.1

Note: From *What a Principal Needs to Know About Interdisciplinary Problem Solving and Inquiry Models* by F. G. Robinson (principal writer), 1988, North Bay, Ontario. Copyright 1988 by Centre for Instructional Leadership. Reprinted by permission.

Making Practical Use of the Interdisciplinary Inquiry Skills List

We believe that the Interdisciplinary Inquiry Skills List can connect problem solving across the disciplines. Thinking and reflecting are significant parts of holistic learning and the examples that follow respond to these aspects. The first few examples will help teachers to apply the IDSL to their particular discipline and thus we can begin to see how the skills can be used in different subjects. These examples are all adaptations of *What a Principal Needs to Know About Interdisciplinary Problem Solving and Inquiry Models* (Robinson, 1988).

Example 1: Applying the IDSL to Inquiry Skills in History

The IDSL can be applied to history to reconstruct events of a period, to compare historical events, or to help solve historical problems. For example, it can be used to answer questions such as, "Which events led to Confederation in 1867?" or, "Compare the Constitution of 1867 with the Act of Union." It can also be used to answer a problem such as, "Should Nova Scotia join the proposed Confederation?" Below the IDSL is applied to this last question.

1. *Establishing a focus for inquiry.* Should Nova Scotia join the proposed Confederation?

2. *Establishing an organizing framework for the focus.* Here the student can develop some courses of action and a set of criteria that roughly correlate with the needs of Nova Scotia's citizens. This can be done in the form of a matrix as illustrated in Table 3.2.

	Join proposed Confederation	Join if ———	Remain Independent
Protection			
Economic cost/benefit			
Sovereignty (self-esteem)			
Cultural (self-enhancement)			

Table 3.2

3. *Identifying sources of information.* The student gathers information from textbooks, period pieces, editorial comments, and literary sources.

4. *Assessing adequacy of information.* Using the information collected, the student assesses the accuracy of data and how closely they follow the original sources. Any possible biases surrounding the data are also examined. In history, for example, historians bring their own perspective to the set of events, in this case Confederation. Finally, the relevance of the data should be examined to see whether the information is related to the framework developed in the second step.

5. *Recording information in the organizing framework.* The data linking the alternatives to the criteria are entered in the cells.

6. *Summarizing information.* The information in each cell is reduced to a summary statement or weights are assigned to criteria.

7. *Observing relationships in summary information.* Determine which alternative is the most valid.

8. *Interpreting relationships observed in the information and making judgments.* Here the student answers the question, "The best course of action for Nova Scotia at this time is. . . ."

9. *Communicating the results.* Students can write an essay organized around the framework:

> + Introduction — what alternatives are being considered; what are the criteria for choosing
> + Body — criterion by criterion comparison of alternatives
> + Summary — statement of alternatives chosen and summary of evidence supporting them.

As stated earlier, developing the organizing framework is the crucial step in the process which guides the student's inquiry through the rest of the process.

Example 2: Applying the IDSL to English

In this example the IDSL is used to help the student construct an essay based on reading a story, "Kid at the Stick."

Interdisciplinary Skills List	Writing Comparative Essays
1. Establishing a focus for the inquiry.	1. In the short story "Kid at the Stick," Frankie, Herb, and Swanson must overcome fear in order to solve a problem. Compare these characters in terms of the reasons for their fear, how they react to their fear, and the results of their reaction on the problem they face.
2. Establishing an organizing framework for the focus.	2. |	Frankie	Herb	Swanson
---	---	---	---
Reasons for fear			
How he reacts to his fear			
The results of his reaction to the problem				 In this representation, the things to be compared are shown as column headings and the basis for comparison (criteria) are shown as row headings.
3. Identifying sources of information (knowing how to locate information at the source, and decoding information at the source).	3. Students go back to the short story and, with the organizer in mind, look for the information that will answer the question. (Some students will be able to recall all of the required information; others will need to go back to the story.)
4. Assessing adequacy of information.	4. To be relevant to the question, only evidence or information that fits the framework need be considered. Students should not include evidence that does not fit under the headings of the framework.
5. Recording information in the organizing framework.	5. |	Frankie	Herb	Swanson
---	---	---	---
Reasons for fear	- his father passed out at the controls of their plane in flight - he is alone - he is afraid to take over the controls for fear of crashing the plane and killing his father and himself			 Students fill in the rest of the framework with the relevant information, as shown above.

6. Summarizing information.	6. (In this case there is no need to summarize information items. However, if we were comparing two books on the criterion "reaction of reviewers," we might summarize ten individual reviewers in the statement "predominantly neutral or mildly positive.")
7. Observing relationships in summary information.	7. Students observe how reactions to fear are linked with consequences in the three instances.
8. Interpreting the relationships observed in the (summary) information and making judgements.	8. In this straightforward continuation of 7, the students would likely make the interpretation that links in 7 are casual, i.e., that different reactions *caused* consequences.
9. Extrapolating the interpretation/judgements beyond the problem's organizing framework.	9. The interpretation, expressed as a proposition ("different people react to fear in different ways, creating different consequences"), would be used by students to understand other "fear" related situations encountered in past or future reading.
10. Communicating the inquiry and its result from the organizing framework.	10. Students would decide upon the manner/ pattern in which to remove the information from the framework in order to answer the original question in essay form. For example: 1. 2. 3. Then they would write an introductory paragraph, three paragraphs in the body of the essay (as circled above), and a concluding paragraph.

In sum, we have presented several examples of how the IDSL might be employed in different school disciplines. By applying these skills in different subjects, students can begin to see how the skills apply to a variety of disciplines and also how the disciplines can be connected through the skills. Thus, these skills, and in particular the frameworking skill, are applicable to a number of subjects. Students eventually gain confidence in using these skills not only in school subjects but also in real-life problems.

Next we turn to how the IDSL can be used to organize problem-solving and inquiry skills instruction across a school division.

Applying the Interdisciplinary Inquiry Skills List

Background Information
You are a teacher in the intermediate division. You realize that your students will become better problem solvers if the inquiry skills they learn in your subject are consistent with what they learn in the other disciplines. You can even imagine teachers from across the subjects getting together to decide how their focus on inquiry skills instruction might be co-ordinated to strengthen a student's learning. The problem is, what model do we select? How can the model fit discipline-specific, problem-solving contexts? Where might we, in our own discipline, build on what is taught in other disciplines? How will my colleagues benefit from what I teach?

A Practical Solution
1. Invite each teacher to study/review the steps in the IDSL.
2. Each teacher then relates objectives from the appropriate Ministry of Education documents for her or his subject to the IDSL (See Figure 3.1).
3. Discuss as an interdisciplinary teaching team the different inquiry skills to be addressed in each discipline. Think about:

      (i)   What particular skills will be emphasized in each discipline.
      (ii)   How the skills will be taught.
      (iii)   When the skills will be taught.
      (iv)   How student growth in these inquiry skills will be diagnosed, monitored, and evaluated.

4. When these questions have been addressed by the interdisciplinary team, invite the team to reflect on what role the IDSL will play in their own subject area, and how the thinking skills "connect" across subjects.

The Topic Development Scheme
Robinson's (Robinson, Ross, & White, 1985) Topic Development Scheme (TDS)

is a practical strategy by which the set of questions a person thinks about when investigating a topic of interest directs the type of inquiry to be pursued. A question about the topic name, for example ("What does the topic name mean?") suggests a Concept Development response; a focus on the course of action to be taken suggests a Decision-Making inquiry, and so forth.

The generic inquiry questions in Table 3.3 below can become the organizers for any intellectual investigation, prompting the type of inquiry required. The inherent strength of the TDS is that it can be taught to students in the junior and intermediate divisions, and they can use it with facility across a range of problem-solving situations.

Generic Inquiry Question	Type of Inquiry
What does the topic name mean?	Concept Development
How does it work?	Model Building
What are changes in characteristics of interest related to?	Correlation
How can I make the characteristics of interest take a desired value?	Causal Analysis
What course of action should be taken?	Decision Making
What steps are necessary to carry out this course of action?	Planning/Procedure

Table 3.3

Complete details on the TDS can be found in Robinson, Ross, and White's *Curriculum Development for Effective Instruction* (1985).

Regarding Table 3.3 above, we note that the generic inquiry question, "What course of action should be taken?" triggers the use of a decision-making inquiry model. This model, with its use of alternatives and criteria, can be used as a way of analyzing past decisions. Florence Maynes (personal communication with the author, 1989) has suggested that in analyses of life's choices, use of the model can result in a clarification of real personal values. For example, why did I choose to go to the movie last night rather than one of the other alternatives available to me (watch television; visit a friend; complete an assigned essay, etc.)? What were the advantages and disadvantages of each alternative that occurred to me? Most importantly, then, what were the guiding considerations that made me choose to go to see the movie? Maynes contends that reviewing the big choices of our lives as well could provide a life story complete with the criteria that guide it.

Cassie and Robinson (1982) suggest the decision-making framework be used as an approach to career choice points. In their article, "A Decision Schema

Approach to Career Decision Making," they explain with practical examples how different career related decisions can be analyzed in terms of the cognitive complexity involved. They present a growth scheme for career related decisions that allows students to make intelligent career choices.

Summary of the OISE Field Services Group Approach

Unquestionably, the OFS group has an impressive accumulation of research, models, curricula strategies, and the like to back their approach to problem solving. However, when reviewed, relative to the contribution the approach makes to the holistic curriculum, some limitations of the system are apparent.

Contribution	Score		
Contribution to Interdisciplinary Linkages	Low	Medium	(High)
Contribution to the Extended Curriculum	(Low)	Medium	High
Contribution to Active Student Learning	Low	(Medium)	High

Table 3.4

The approach, with its Interdisciplinary Skills List and Topic Development Scheme, provides excellent support for linking instruction across the disciplines. However, as shown in Table 3.4, this problem-solving system scores low to medium on its contribution to the extended curriculum since intuition and creativity are not included explicitly in the model. It should be noted, however, that a new model of an intentional holistic learner is being developed which includes intuition in its problem-solving approach. Finally, the OFS group's approach to teaching problem solving addresses, to a large extent, the active role of the learner.

THE CREATIVE PROBLEM-SOLVING MODEL

Creative Problem Solving, authored by Scott G. Isaksen and Donald J. Treffinger (1985), is based on the widely known Osborn-Parnes Creative Problem-Solving (CPS) model (Parnes, 1984). The former authors comment on their use of the Osborn-Parnes model in this way:

> We have found this model has been very powerful in guiding our research, writing, teaching and consulting... the... model has provided a sound and productive framework for our efforts....
>
> We hope [our model] will... also be a valid and contemporary restatement of the Osborn-Parnes model. (pp. 1, 7)

There are six major components or stages in the CPS process. These are:

Mess-Finding. This initial stage involves probing one's interests, experiences, and concerns — the starting points for CPS. Of central importance in this stage is knowing how to choose, establish priorities, or select a general focus for creative problem solving.

Data-Finding. Here the problem solver tunes into all available information, knowledge, facts, feelings, thoughts, opinions, or questions about the Mess. Emphasis at this stage is on clarification of the Mess.

Problem-Finding. In this stage, an attempt is made to refocus the "problem" into a number of problems or sub-problems. This refocusing is possible only if the problem solver reserves judgement and consciously attempts to expand the problem space to the reasonable limits of the Mess and its associated data.

Idea-Finding. The focus at this stage is on generating many ideas and alternatives using creative search methods. The alternatives are stimulated by the problem statement(s) of the previous stage.

Solution-Finding. The problem solver thinks about how the alternatives address the problem(s). Criteria are elicited to provide a rational basis for analyzing promising ideas systematically.

Acceptance-Finding. The goal here is to take the problem-solving possibilities and consider specific elements of them which will promote successful implementation. From this stage comes a step-by-step plan of action.

It should be noted that the apparent simplicity of the CPS model is misleading. The model is far from a linear, lock-step sequencing of a skills or task list. In practice, the model has found ready acceptance in business, industry, and segments of the educational community. Recent extensions of this model are being used in courses designed for gifted elementary and secondary school students.

At each stage, Isaksen and Treffinger emphasize the importance of there being a dynamic balance between *divergence* and *convergence*. In the divergent mode, the problem solver is encouraged to search, to seek many possibilities, and to stretch her or his thinking. In the equally important convergent phase, efforts are made to focus the process by screening, selecting, and choosing the most important or promising possibilities. Ground rules for each of these phases are provided by the authors.

In their text, entitled *Creative Problem Solving: The Basic Course,* the above authors provide a historical background to their model, a self-instructional approach to each stage and phase of the model, numerous strategies that facilitate the process, and a number of sample applications of the model. Below is an example of how the CPS model can be applied to an interdisciplinary problem.

PROBLEM: *What type of immigration policy should Canada have regarding refugees?*

CPS:

1. *Mess-Finding.*   Mess-Finding strategies would involve talking about the problems facing refugees, what prompts them to come to Canada, and the effects of allowing refugees into Canada. Students could try putting themselves in the position of a refugee. In the convergent phase students begin to focus more specifically on the Mess, and develop some initial thoughts about a plan to look at the problem. However, at this point no detailed plan is developed.

2. *Data-Finding.*   At this stage there is an opportunity to explore a variety of subjects in relation to the problem. For example, students in the divergent mode can read case studies of refugees from different cultures. Case studies can focus on economic, religious, and political repression. Literature and art that is related to the experiences of refugees can also be brought into the investigation. In addition, students can examine statistics such as those found in the following data report (cited in Bondy, 1983, p. 34).

> *Spaceship Earth*
> If the world is the equivalent of a village of 100:
> 6   = North Americans with 1/2 of the world's income
> 70 = unable to read
> 1   = college education
> 50 = suffering malnutrition to some degree
> 50 = without safe or adequate water supply
> 80 = living in substandard housing

The students should explore their own feelings and experiences regarding the problems of refugees. For example, have they met or talked with a refugee (e.g., a Vietnamese boat person)? In the convergent phase, the students sift through the data explored and identify the crucial issues and information.

3. *Problem-Finding.*   In this step the students develop a number of problem statements, such as: What responsibility does Canada have to refugees from other countries? How will refugees fit into the Canadian mosaic or our vision of

Canada?   What rights does a refugee have?   After developing a number of questions, the students develop a working problem statement in the convergent phase, such as: What is fair policy for admitting refugees into Canada?

4. *Idea-Finding*. Here the students develop a number of alternatives in response to the question. Alternatives could focus on exploring a range of possibilities, from an open-door policy to a very restrictive policy with a narrow definition of what constitutes a refugee. From the range of alternatives developed, the students come up with one they find acceptable. For example, the students might select a relatively open policy with a broad definition of what constitutes a refugee.

5. *Solution-Finding*. The students now develop criteria to examine the selected alternative. Criteria might include determining if the policy adequately takes into account the rights of the refugee, the impact of an open policy on Canada's economy and social life, and if the response is adequate from the point of view of the world as an interdependent global village. In the convergent phase these criteria are refined and then applied to the solution to assess the overall strengths and weaknesses of the proposed solution. In developing and applying the criteria there is another opportunity to apply an interdisciplinary focus by drawing on political, economic, literary, and religious sources.

6. *Acceptance-Finding*. The students can now look at the effects of implementing the policy that they have selected. For example, students could look at factors that would facilitate or hinder the implementation of the relatively open policy proposed. Based on this initial exploration, students can try to develop a specific plan of action in the convergent phase of this step.

Summary of the Creative Problem-Solving Model
The CPS model has many strengths when evaluated in terms of its potential for interdisciplinary contributions to the holistic curriculum. Central to the Mess-Finding stage, for example, is the selection of a general focus which counters the tendency of novice problem solvers to apply ill-conceived solution strategies when they misrepresent the problem in the beginning. As the adage says, "If you don't know where you're going, you're likely to end up somewhere else."

In CPS, one is encouraged to wallow both cognitively and affectively in the problem situation, to become fully sensitized to the problem being explored. The authors (Miller Cassie, and Drake) see this approach of reserving judgement as a significant contribution to one's creativity. MacKinnon (1978) is quoted as saying, for example, that "creative persons are especially open to experience, both of the inner self and of the outer world... they are open to and receptive of experience" (p. 129). Moreover, as the problem solver confronts the so-called

Mess, she or he immerses herself or himself in the problem, resisting any temptation to define it prematurely. Through a divergent "openness to experience" phase, the mind is prepared for a convergent phase out of which comes appropriate direction.

If students are encouraged to *resolve* problems before being fully aware of the dimensions of the Mess, several things can happen. Initially, the students may experience a short-lived sense of tension reduction and satisfaction in defining the problem. This sense of satisfaction, or even exhilaration, may continue for some time after the problem-solving sequence has been completed. However, the hoped-for result usually does not materialize, at least to the anticipated extent: the test result is lower than expected; the problem persists; or the problem returns in a modified form.

More fundamentally, premature closure in the Mess-Finding stage may rob the problem solvers of relevant knowledge. This knowledge may not be accessed because the early "fixing" of the problem can limit the conscious and unconscious search for relevant information. In other words, if you do not sense a need for a more powerful introduction to your short story, you are unlikely to search for the means by which the introduction can be replaced or enriched. Similarly, if in solving a problem in physics your initial representation of the problem elements does not include the effect of friction on the moving object, you are not likely to introduce your previously learned understanding of friction in your problem resolution. Isaksen and Treffinger have very wisely responded to premature problem representation by proposing a balance between divergence and convergence, and letting the problem elements become fully experienced by the problem solver.

In the Data-Finding phase, Isaksen and Treffinger include both cognitive and affective information. According to these authors, "the purpose of data-finding is to help you explore all the information, impressions, observations, feelings, and questions that you have about a mess on which you've decided to work" (p. Four-1). The problem solver not only looks at information, but also examines feelings, intuitions, beliefs, desires, and doubts. This is a second notable contribution of the model: the user is encouraged to apply both experience-expanding and logic-synthesizing skills. The model challenges those who teach problem solving to consider the limitations of mere logical analysis. A further contribution is the focus on breaking away from fixed patterns of thought and action that may limit the emergence of creative solutions. Putting a check on "the old ways of doing it" opens the mind to the possibility of creating new patterns and solutions.

The Acceptance-Finding stage also makes a considerable contribution to problem solving. Here one considers potential problems associated with the implementation of the solution. For example, during the early 1960s, someone suggested that the best way to remove the lamprey eel menace from the Great Lakes was to drain the Great Lakes. The impracticality of this solution would be "checked" in several stages of the Isaksen and Treffinger model; however, should this solution be carried forward from the Solution-Finding stage, it would undoubtedly receive ambitious scrutiny in the final Acceptance-Finding phase.

Using the comparison chart with which the OFS group's approach was analyzed in Table 3.4, we find the CPS model contributes to the holistic curriculum as shown below in Table 5:

Contribution   **Score**

Contribution to Interdisciplinary Linkages	(Low)	Medium	High
Contribution to the Extended Curriculum	Low	Medium	(High)
Contribution to Active Student Learning	Low	Medium	(High)

Table 3.5

The CPS model reviewed in this chapter can be adapted to suit problem-solving activities across disciplines. Nevertheless, the authors do not claim to relate the model to the discipline-specific inquiries or to the discipline-specific inquiry language that appears in course guidelines. For these reasons, we consider the model's contribution to interdisciplinary linkage low.

However, the CPS model makes a considerable contribution to extended curriculum in that it promotes the intuitive and creative processes as described earlier. It encourages problem solvers to track their visceral awareness and to experience both incongruity and "dis-ease" in the problem definition phase. In so doing, the model stresses more than mere cognition.

Relative to the active learning criterion, the CPS model's contribution is deemed "high." At each stage of the model the user must remain active. In Mess-Finding, the user probes her or his interests, experiences, and concerns, clearly an active orientation. In Data-Finding, the problem solver explores feelings, thoughts, and opinions about the so-called Mess. Similarly, throughout the entire process, the person using this approach remains both affectively and cognitively engaged by the process. It is through this active learning aspect of the CPS process that the model can become transformational. Nevertheless, the manner in which the model is taught and engaged by the learner will determine whether it is used in a mechanistic manner or in an experientially rich, creative way.

Since the CPS model was not designed specifically for school subjects and academic disciplines, it requires some adapting to a curricular context. But, the CPS model provides a logical extension to the Dewey model (1933) of reflective reasoning, and the general problem-solving model that currently appears in the Ontario Ministry of Education's Research Study Skills (1979) document. Its steps and sub-routines clearly contribute to the growth and development of students' problem-solving skills. Below are some exercises that can be integrated with the CPS model. The first exercise, for example, can be used in the initial steps to stimulate creativity and engage the student in the process.

Exercise I
Title: Exploring Personal Blocks

Objective: *to review students' potential personal blocks to creativity; to relate personal blocks to experiences students have faced or might face in problem-solving contexts.*

Instructions:
1. Inform students that "a creative mind" is a mind open to experience, a mind that is free to think about new and different ways of doing things: "The exercise we're about to do will help us think about certain personal obstacles that block our creativity." In problem solving, we have found that a creative mind can assist the problem solver at every phase of the problem-solving process.

2. Provide each student with Worksheet #1. Invite students to work in pairs. Each pair is to read the seven blocks to creativity and then complete their explanation of what the blocks mean.

3. When students have "defined" the seven blocks, circulate Worksheet #2 which provides another definition or explanation of the blocks to creativity.

4. After student pairs have compared their initial "definitions" with those on Worksheet #2, invite them to complete the third column on Worksheet #2: "How this block may be affecting my problem solving in my school subjects."

5. The exercise concludes with students relating personal blocks to their success (or frustration) in solving problems in their various school subjects (example: English, science, mathematics, geography, history, art and/or other electives).

6. (Optional) Students could explore strategies for overcoming personal blocks. To assist with this exploration, they may want to ask the questions: "How did I get this block?" "Why does it persist?" "What can I do about it?"

Worksheet #1

Personal Blocks	What I think this block is (as it relates to me solving problems)
1. Self-confidence.	1.
2. My need to be like others.	2.
3. My old habits.	3.
4. Lack of interest.	4.
5. Lack of experience.	5.
6. My need for speed.	6.
7. My tendency to distrust my feelings.	7.

Worksheet #2 This exercise is particularly appropriate for the Problem-Finding stage.

Personal Blocks	Explanations	How this block may be affecting my problem solving in my school subjects.
1. Self-confidence.	Often we lack confidence in ourselves as problem solvers. When we need to solve a problem, therefore, we doubt ourselves and think we can't do it. When we feel this way, it's hard to be imaginative and motivated.	1.
2. My need to be like others.	Sometimes we know how someone else would solve the problem so we don't even try to come up with our own approach(es). We limit our imaginative range by accepting another person's way of thinking.	2.
3. My old habits.	We may get accustomed to handling problems in a certain way. As a result, we don't even consider other (perhaps better) ways of handling problems.	3.
4. Lack of interest.	In our lack of interest we can affect our motivation. Therefore, we don't try to use our minds and our senses to come up with intelligent, creative responses.	4.
5. Lack of experience.	You can find a problem hard to address or deal with if the situation is new or unfamiliar to you.	5.

6. My need for speed.	Sometimes we hurry through a problem without stopping to consider the problem we're working with. When we feel rushed, we don't always tune in to what our imaginations and our senses are telling us.	6.
7. My tendency to distrust my feelings.	Our feelings and emotions can help us tap our creative energy. When we *think* but fail to tune in to *how we feel*, we often miss what our experience is "telling" us.	7.

Exercise II
Title: The Open Mind

Objective: *to help students "stretch" their data collection skills.*

Instructions:
1. Invite all students to stand and to clasp their hands behind their backs.
2. When students are standing with hands behind their backs (as you are yourself, modelling the behaviour), ask students to:

"Think about yourself as an observer.
Ask yourself whether or not you notice details."

Then mention that solving problems often requires careful analysis of details.
3. With the students still standing, ask all students who are wearing wrist watches to remain standing with their hands clasped behind their backs. The rest of the class can sit down quietly.
4. Now, mention to students that "in a typical day, researchers claim, we look at our watch about 14 times. In a year we observe our watch 5110 times on average! Let's see how much you have observed about your watches:

(a) Is the face round, square, or what?
(b) What does it say in words on the face?
(c) Does it have numbers or is it digital?
(d) Describe your watch in detail.

Now, look at your watch and see if it is as you described it.

After students with watches have compared their thoughts with reality, have them clasp their hands behind their backs. Ask each student what time it is on her or his watch (no peeking!). Many will be surprised that they did not notice the time while looking at their watches.

"This activity demonstrates how we see (and remember) selectively. Sometimes, when our minds are not open to all the detail available to us, we fail to perceive important information. Good observation skills assist us in problem solving, especially in the data collection phase."

5. Next, place an object on your desk in front of the classroom. Invite students to describe the object in writing. After five minutes, have several student descriptions read.

Then, invite students to describe the object using the table below:

SEE What does it look like?	TASTE How does it taste?	SMELL How does it smell?
HEAR Does it create sound?	TOUCH/FEEL How does it feel?	OTHER (Anything else?)

Table 3.6

After five minutes, invite students to describe the object using the chart as a "trigger." Compare the two sets of descriptions:

In what ways are they similar?
Any differences?
Why?

6. Explain that our brains are stimulated by messages received by our senses. Our minds process these sensory messages. When we fail to acknowledge these messages we limit the "incoming" information and rob the mind of its ability to process the rich data base to which we are exposed.

7. Students can work in small groups (three to five per group) to discuss how the powers of observation can facilitate problem solving in the various disciplines.

Exercise III
Title: Forced Fit

Objective: *to increase originality in thought (by finding relationships between objects and events that are not typically associated).*

Instructions:
1. Read the following situation to students (place it on an overhead for viewing as you read):

> Chris has had considerable difficulty making friends. Students in the new school seem distant and uninterested in anything Chris does. What might Chris do to improve the situation?

2. Invite students to brainstorm for possibilities.

3. Next, have the students think about each of the following objects which are not usually associated with this situation. Ask the students to suggest ways in which each object could help Chris with the above situation.

> (a) A flashlight.
> (b) A book of poems.
> (c) A photocopy machine.
> (d) A can of pepper.
> (e) A 1961 edition of *Life Magazine.*

This last exercise is most applicable to the Idea-Finding stage, in which students are seeking a creative solution.

4. The above activity will be difficult at first for many students. Once students click into their "creative mode" they tend to surprise themselves and others with the intelligent, creative responses they generate.

Invite students to share their responses in small groups of three to five. When the sharing activity has continued for about 15 minutes, regroup. Ask the class to comment on their experiences with this exercise:

> (a) How might your learning from this exercise assist you in problem solving? Give examples.
> (b) How might your learning apply to problem solving in your school subjects? Give examples.

Suggestions:
If students require assistance with moving into the creative realm, suggest how an item such as a penknife might be the object of creative focus. For instance:

> + when thinking of a penknife, a person might conjure up images of a grandfather who gave her or him a penknife for her or his 10th birthday;
> + a birthday, in turn, suggests a party;
> + a party makes the student think about how Chris could take a proactive role and plan an interesting party to which potential friends could be invited.

Thus a totally unrelated item triggered a creative idea about how to address the problem at hand.

WALLAS MODEL

The model developed by Graham Wallas (1926) emphasizes the processes of incubation and illumination and combines them with analytic thought. The seven-stage model described below is a modification of the original four-step model (Miller, 1988). An example based on the Meech Lake Accord is also included.

Uncertainty/Ambiguity. Most problem solving is prompted by an unresolved situation. This stage is similar to the Mess-Finding stage.   Regarding our example of Meech Lake, the uncertainty involved leaving Québéc out of the constitutional agreement signed in 1982. The Meech Lake Accord would have brought Québéc into the constitution, but some critics (e.g., Trudeau) felt that it would have reduced federal power too much.

Problem Clarification. In this step, the person or group attempts to get some sort of handle on the problem. This task might be accomplished by writing out a problem statement. Unlike logical mathematical problem solving, the problem statement is not a hypothesis in the technical sense; instead, it attempts to get at the root of the problem. Imagery and intuition can be used at this stage to help sort out the problem; by inner reflection the central issue may come forth.
        The problem in our example is: should the Meech Lake Accord have been signed?

Preparation/Frameworking. Here one attempts to develop a more complete framework for the problem as one tries to see the problem from a broader perspective than that found in the previous step. This step tends to involve more linear thinking as each aspect of the framework is explored; however, imagery and intuition can still play a role here. It is possible, for example, for one to have an image of either part of the framework or a vision of the entire approach.

In our example, this step involves looking closely at the provisions of the Accord and at one's vision of Canada. Students can first develop their own visions of Canada. For example, do they see the country run by a strong central government which can determine the course of action regarding issues such as control of oil reserves, the administration of health care systems, etc.? Or, alternatively, do they see Canada as more decentralized, with the provinces having a strong say in these issues? A variety of sources from different subjects could be used here. Students could do some visualization about how they see Canada and also how they see various ethnic and minority groups and women as part of the social fabric. After working through their own visions, they can look closely at the provisions in the Meech Lake Accord so that they understand what was proposed.

Incubation. Incubation involves standing back and letting the elements work themselves through at a subconscious level. If the problem-solving process is forced too much, it will become less productive. Incubation can occur throughout the problem-solving process. In fact, although these steps are presented in a linear order, the approach we are describing is really much more fluid and is not a step-by-step process.

In the Meech Lake example let the students step back from the problem for awhile. They can discuss the issues involved, but it can be helpful just to let things sit for awhile as the students let their sense of both Canada, and the relation of the Accord to their visions, develop.

Alternative Search. This stage usually involves a more conscious search for and examination of alternatives. Alternative courses of action are first explored and developed, and then judged against criteria. These criteria can be developed consciously and can include either a number of factors, or only a few which are felt more intuitively. Ultimately, these criteria are usually related to the framework. It is also possible that examining alternatives can change the original framework. Again this whole problem-solving process tends to move back-and-forth, rather than follow a logical sequence.

The students deal with the Meech Lake issue more consciously as they clarify their visions and compare them with the Accord. Students can be asked, "In what ways does the Accord match your vision and in what ways does it not?" The students can approach this question systematically by writing out their visions and listing the provisions with which they agree and those with which they disagree. Their visions provide the criteria for assessing the Accord.

Alternative Selection/Illumination. Here the person settles on a course of action. This step can involve a rational assessment of the alternatives placed against the criteria, or it may evolve through the appearance of an image. If an image or intuitive insight does occur, it can also be assessed against the criteria, but we have to be careful that our criteria and mind-set do not become too rigid. If the criteria are too inflexible, creativity will be stifled. If the vision is a powerful one, the criteria themselves may have to be reworked.

In our example, the students decide whether or not they would actually sign the Accord. After the more systematic alternative search, the students can step back again and do some inner reflection (e.g., a short meditation) on the decision. Following the inner reflection there is a greater chance that the decision will not be an abstract one, but one that is more connected to the whole person. The students can then write down their decisions and the reasons for them.

Verification. Now the solution must be tested by verifying through feedback the quality of the idea, or simply by trying out the solution.

In our example, students sharing their answers with other students and with the teacher in this last step. They can also compare their solutions to other responses to the Accord.

Summary of the Wallas Model

In general, the Wallas model shares the same application to the holistic curriculum as CPS, as shown in Table 3.7.

Contribution   **Score**

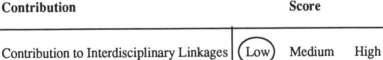

Contribution to Interdisciplinary Linkages	Low	Medium	High
Contribution to the Extended Curriculum	Low	Medium	High
Contribution to Active Student Learning	Low	Medium	High

(Low is circled in first row; High is circled in second and third rows)

Table 3.7

Since the Wallas model is transdisciplinary, the teacher would have to develop the links between various subjects. We regard the essential strength of the Wallas model as being its contribution to the extended curriculum. As described above, the model lends itself to visualizing exercises, tuning in to one's "experiencing," and reflecting through meditation. Throughout these activities, the student's active involvement in the problem-solving process is heightened.

A Final Problem-Solving Exercise

Background Information:
Marzano (1985, 1985a) describes two approaches to learning-to-learn, one being the teaching of a practical set of steps to follow when students engage a learning activity (sometimes called a "heuristic" approach by cognitive psychologists); the other is the focusing on specific points in the thinking "cycle" such as goal-setting, attention, self-evaluation, and so forth. This exercise represents a combination of these two approaches.

Instructions:
The proposed strategy is designed to help students increase awareness of their learning process. Many students will find the exercise relaxes them, focuses their thoughts and feelings on their present learning, and invites them to tune-in more deliberately to how they learn best.

For this exercise to work, students must be informed that the exercise requires their full co-operation and attention. Since the exercise involves a meditative component and guidance from the teacher, anything less than total group support for the exercise will almost certainly threaten its success. Nevertheless, when students willingly attempt the learning strategy, most students benefit from the experience and continue to apply the strategy without teacher interventions.

Step 1: Relaxation
To begin the exercise, students should be quiet and attentive. They are invited to sit comfortably as a relaxation routine is begun. Soft music, mental imagery, muscular relaxation routines, and so forth may assist with this step. The focus here is on helping students relax so that they can concentrate on subsequent steps in the process.

Step 2: Focusing
In this step, students are invited to think about and experience —

(a)	where they are and why they are here;
(b)	their feelings about being in this class at this time;
(c)	their concentration — how tuned-in they are, right now, to themselves;
(d)	their sense of how involved they are in learning in this classroom;
(e)	their belief in themselves, their capability, and their worth.

Step 3: Assuming Responsibility
Now students are asked to dig deeper into —

(a)   what they can learn by being a student in this class;
(b)   what this class is all about;
(c)   how they can tune-in more fully to the class and how they can exert more energy.

Invite students to "be" this kind of student: "Picture yourself the way you want to be in this class."

Step 4: Goal-Setting
At this point, students have experienced themselves as successful, energized, tuned-in students. The visualization from Step 3 is now moved into a goal-setting phase in which students —

(a)   think about what they need to do to be the student they wish to be;
(b)   talk to themselves about the goals they are now setting for their performance as students.

Step 5: Steps to Growth
After Step 4, students are ready to "return" to the more routine classroom agenda. It is at this point that they are invited to make concrete what they were feeling, thinking, saying to themselves, and visualizing in the relaxed state above. Now, they are asked to —

(a)   think about their performance to date in this class;
(b)   think about the gap between what they have achieved and what they would like to achieve;
(c)   consider what specific steps they need to take if they are to take seriously the decision to change;
(d)   identify the assistance they will need from classmates, the teacher, and others if their change goals are to be realized.

Step 6: Monitoring and Self-Assessment
The exercise is incomplete without attention being paid to the actual changes in their thoughts, feelings, and behaviours. Students need to be aware of themselves over time to determine —

(a)   Were their goals reached?
(b)   What worked, what did not, and why?

(c)   What did they learn about themselves, and do they like what they have learned?

(d)   How are their focusing, commitment, and effort different from what they were?

The inherent strength of the above exercise is its meta-cogitative focus. By focusing on themselves as learners in the process of learning, students are participating in a reflective experience that can result in better grades across all disciplines. Moreover, since the approach employs the application of problem-solving skills to students' exploration of their inner experience, it promotes transcendence, a significant aspect of the transformational orientation.

CHAPTER REVIEW

Over the past 20 years, the "structured" (schema-based) and the "creative" problem-solving models have each developed a sizable following among North American educators. However, many people have come to believe that a commitment to holistic education requires that these separate models now be synthesized into a more comprehensive account of human functioning in problematic situations.

At the present time, a group comprising many of the people who contributed to the developments described in this chapter has been formed for the purpose of achieving this synthesis. The starting point is a jointly developed model for "the intentional holistic learner." When existing problem-solving models are plotted on this conception, it can be seen that they selectively engage particular components of the total human psyche. The ambitious intent of the synthesis is to draw in *all* critical components.

While this synthesis is not yet complete, it has reached a stage of development that allows a fresh approach to the construction of strategies for human functioning in complex problematic situations. For example, the model recognizes that the intentional holistic learner does not typically deal with isolated or "novel" problems. Rather, this individual has continuing concerns, vitally connected with the human needs hierarchy, that recur throughout life in an expanding range of significant contexts. Consequently, a problem-solving model that is to connect the present problem to the individual's life experience — the highest form of personal integration — must come to grips with how human learners deal with topics of continuing interest, and how they build upon what they already know about such topics.

As an example, in many Canadian high schools today the Meech Lake Accord is presented as a problem for students to discuss and reach some conclusion about. In some of the "structured" problem-solving models discussed earlier, this problem would be cast in a decision matrix, whose alternatives are, "ratify Accord as is" or "do not ratify Accord as is," and whose criteria would be such things as "effect on national unity," and so on. While students would fill in such matrices and reach a "reasoned conclusion," the Meech Lake problem remains so remote from their personal experience that the estimates of its effects may reflect little more than the political rhetoric of the groups with which students align themselves.

On the other hand, approaches that stress creativity would invite students to brainstorm about or envisage optimal relations between the federal government and the provinces. While this would encourage the students to use their intuition and creativity, their responses need have no vital connection to the knowledge schema they have built up from experience and learning. Consequently, we have no more assurance that the product will have quality or utility than we have when structured models are used.

In the new problem-solving models, learners would be encouraged to consider the particular problem as an instance of a more general type of problem with which they have already had experience. For this example, this general problem might be described as, "the optimal distribution of authority among hierarchically organized groups of rule makers." This is a pervasive human problem which will have been encountered first in the family context (parent/child authority relationships), then in the school context (teacher/student authority relationships), and then in the provincial context (the division of power between provincial and municipal governments).

Undoubtedly, students will know the family context best; indeed, they will have constructed a "model" of how authority relationships "work" in the family, that is, a mental map of elements and relationships in this particular hierarchically organized group of rule makers. In this model they will find simple, clear examples of all the key concepts of the Meech Lake debate: (family) unity, individual rights, opting out, veto, and even transfer payments all have a concrete meaning in the family context. Students will have developed an understanding that rules must, in fairness, be differentially applied to individual members because of their unequal resources, their different experiences (histories), or their particular needs. They will have strong, experience-based feelings about such matters as what constitutes equitable treatment of such individuals, and the threatened or actual "separation" of a member from the rest of the family.

It is in connection with the most familiar example of the general problem that the process of visualization can be used to its best advantage. Anyone who has lived in a family can envisage changes in the way it works that would lead to the greater satisfaction of members' needs. In other words, the visualization of potential alternative futures need not be an artificial abstract exercise. It is experience-based creative projections that provide the substance for the ultimate phase of the problem-solving episode — choosing among quality alternatives.

The person trying to come to grips with the Meech Lake Accord would progressively extend the model that took shape in the family context into the school and provincial settings, adding new elements and relationships as they are revealed by reflection on past personal experience in these settings. From this experience, the student would acquire a sense of how the dominant principles — such as equity, or realizing the greatest benefit to the largest number of people — that were used to resolve rule-making disputes in these familiar contexts, could be applied in the national context.

Although the reader will be able to retrieve from this account the main threads of a strategy for dealing with problems that recur in a succession of life contexts, we think it would be premature to write down a detailed set of steps. Our intention here is to demonstrate that it is possible to devise strategies that engage and draw together complex cognitive structures, strongly held feelings, the human capacity for invention (creativity), and a broad segment of life experience.

While we have not demonstrated it in this account, it can be shown that the success of such "super-strategies" rests on the prior acquisition of the much simpler strategies that we have described earlier in this chapter. The task for teachers, then, is not to abandon these less complex strategies, but to accelerate their appearance and consolidation in our schools. When this has been accomplished, intermediate and senior grade students can be taught schemes that allow the engagement of "life problems" in their full complexity.

REFERENCES

Anderson, J. (1982). Acquisition of cognitive skills, *Psychological Review, 89*, 369-406.

Anderson, J. (1983). *The architecture of cognition.* Cambridge, MA: Harvard University Press.

Bondy, R. J. (1983). *Canada: Windows on the world.* Toronto: Prentice-Hall.

Boulding, K. E. (1981). The future of general systems. In A. M. White (Ed.), *New directions for teaching and learning: Interdisciplinary teaching 8* (pp. 27-34). San Francisco: Jossey-Bass.

Buber, M. (1947). *Between Man and Man.* London: Kegan Paul, Trench, Trubner.

Cassie, J. R. B., & Robinson, F. G. (1982, Summer). A decision schema approach to career decision making. *International Journal for the Advancement of Counselling, 5*(3), 60-78.

Chance, P. (1986). *Thinking in the classroom: A survey of programs.* New York: Teachers College Press.

Dewey, J. (1933). *How we think.* Boston: D. E. Heath.

Isaksen, S. G., & Treffinger, D. J. (1985). *Creative problem solving: The basic course.* Buffalo, NY: Bearly.

Mackinnon, D. (1978). *In search of human effectiveness: Identifying and developing creativity.* Buffalo, NY: Bearly.

Markely, O. W. (1987, Second Quarter). Using depth intuition in creative problem solving and strategic innovation. *The Journal of Creative Behavior,* 22(2), 85-101.

Marzano, R. (1985a). *The systematic teaching and reinforcing of thinking and reasoning skills within content area classrooms.* Denver: Mid-Continent Regional Educational Library.

Marzano, R. (1985, June). *Integrated instruction in thinking skills, learning strategies, traditional content and basic beliefs: A necessary unit.* Education Resources Information Centre, #ED267906, pp. 1-39 (PS D15 704).

Miller, J. P. (1988). *The Holistic Curriculum.* Toronto: OISE Press.

Nickerson, R. S., Perkins, D. N., & Smith, E. E. (1985). *The teaching of thinking.* Hillsdale, NJ: Lawrence Erlbaum Associates.

Ontario Ministry of Education. (1975). *Research study skills.* Toronto: Ministry of Education

Ontario Ministry of Education. (1980, June). *Issues and directions.* Toronto: Ministry of Education.

Ontario Ministry of Education. (1986). *History and contemporary studies.* Toronto: Ministry of Education.

Ontario Ministry of Education. (1988). *Geography: Intermediate and senior divisions.* Toronto: Ministry of Education.

Parnes, S. J. (1984). *The magic of your mind.* Buffalo, NY: Bearly.

Robinson, F. G. (1988, Summer). *What a principal needs to know about interdisciplinary problem solving and inquiry models.* Paper prepared for use at the Midnorthern-Northeastern Principals' Course, Northeastern Field Centre, Ontario Institute for Studies in Education, North Bay, Ontario.

Robinson, F. G., Ross, J. A., & White, F. (1985). *Curriculum development for effective instruction.* Toronto: OISE Press.

Ross, J. A., & Maynes, F. A. (1982). *Teaching problem solving.* Toronto: OISE Press.

Segal, J. W., Chipman, S. F., & Glaser, R. (Eds.). (1985). *Thinking and learning skills: Vol. 1. Relating instruction to research.* Hillsdale, NJ: Lawrence Erlbaum Associates.

Wallas, G. (1926). *The art of thought.* London: Waits.

CHAPTER 4

DEVELOPING UNITS IN INTEGRATED STUDIES

In this chapter we discuss some basic considerations regarding developing units in integrated studies. Unit design can facilitate the integration of subject matter if the objectives, teaching strategies, resources, and evaluation techniques involved in unit development are approached from a holistic perspective. One should also keep in mind the three orientations (transmission, transaction, and transformation) and how they can affect the various components of unit development. As an initial organizer, Table 4.1 is presented to show how teaching strategies and evaluation procedures can shift with the different perspectives. This table will be referred to throughout the chapter. In examining this table, it is important to remember the possible relationships among the three orientations. Thus, if we see the positions as increasingly more inclusive, the transformation position would include some of the strategies associated with the other two positions. A transformation-oriented teacher might lecture and use conventional evaluation techniques as well as guided imagery and self-evaluation through the use of journals. However, the transformation teacher tends to teach from the Self, or big fellow (see p. 3). The transformation teacher's lecture is not rooted in the transfer of information, but instead attempts to connect with the student's Self by using stories, images, and metaphor. With these considerations in mind, we will now discuss the components of unit development.

OBJECTIVES

Elliot Eisner (1985) has discussed different types of objectives which are relevant to the three positions. One type of objective is the instructional objective which specifies "unambiguously the particular behaviour (skill, item of knowledge and so forth) the student is to acquire after having completed one or more learning activities" (p. 53). Instructional objectives, then, tend to be transmissional. An example of an instructional objective might be: "the student will be able to write a clear definition of 'time' at the end of the unit." Integrated studies will contain instructional objectives since there will be clear expectations for students within the units. It is important to recognize that integrated studies does not preclude clearly defined objectives.

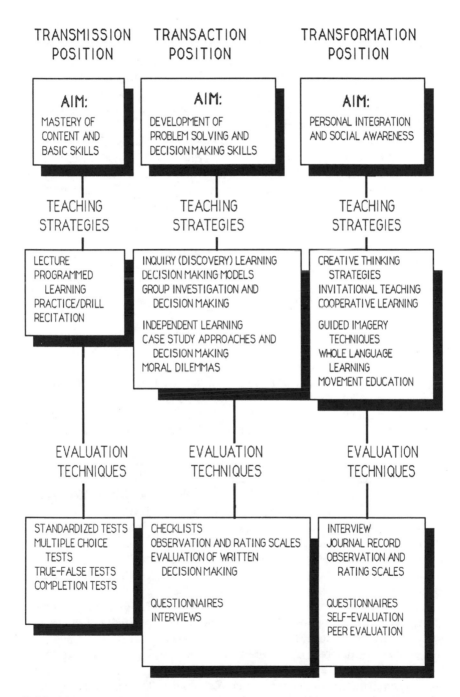

TRANSMISSION
POSITION

AIM:
MASTERY OF
CONTENT AND
BASIC SKILLS

TEACHING
STRATEGIES

LECTURE
PROGRAMMED
LEARNING
PRACTICE/DRILL
RECITATION

EVALUATION
TECHNIQUES

STANDARDIZED TESTS
MULTIPLE CHOICE
TESTS
TRUE-FALSE TESTS
COMPLETION TESTS

TRANSACTION
POSITION

AIM:
DEVELOPMENT OF
PROBLEM SOLVING AND
DECISION MAKING SKILLS

TEACHING
STRATEGIES

INQUIRY (DISCOVERY) LEARNING
DECISION MAKING MODELS
GROUP INVESTIGATION AND
DECISION MAKING

INDEPENDENT LEARNING
CASE STUDY APPROACHES AND
DECISION MAKING
MORAL DILEMMAS

EVALUATION
TECHNIQUES

CHECKLISTS
OBSERVATION AND RATING SCALES
EVALUATION OF WRITTEN
DECISION MAKING

QUESTIONNAIRES
INTERVIEWS

TRANSFORMATION
POSITION

AIM:
PERSONAL INTEGRATION
AND SOCIAL AWARENESS

TEACHING
STRATEGIES

CREATIVE THINKING
STRATEGIES
INVITATIONAL TEACHING
COOPERATIVE LEARNING

GUIDED IMAGERY
TECHNIQUES
WHOLE LANGUAGE
LEARNING
MOVEMENT EDUCATION

EVALUATION
TECHNIQUES

INTERVIEW
JOURNAL RECORD
OBSERVATION AND
RATING SCALES

QUESTIONNAIRES
SELF-EVALUATION
PEER EVALUATION

Table 4.1

Eisner also identifies another type of objective which he calls a Type III objective. A Type III objective is characterized by a specific problem which can have several types of solutions. Thus, the architect or engineer may have a very specific context to work in, but will not be limited to one solution. Students could study the traffic patterns around their school, for example, and seek to improve the flow and safety of traffic. Since the Type III objective often focuses on problem solving, it tends to be transactional.

A third type is what Eisner calls an expressive objective. An expressive objective does not specify behaviours, but describes an educational encounter: "It identifies a situation in which children are to work, a problem with which they are to cope, a task in which they are to engage" (p. 54). The expectation of the expressive objective is not homogeneity of response, but diversity. Examples of expressive objectives are:

1. To interpret the meaning of *Paradise Lost*.

2. To examine and appraise the significance of *The Old Man and The Sea*.

3. To develop a three-dimensional form through the use of wire and wood. (Eisner, 1985, p. 55)

Expressive objectives tend to be transformational in nature because they encourage diversity and creativity in the student's response.

In designing integrated studies units, then, it is possible to have instructional, expressive, and Type III objectives. Whatever the type of objective, it should still promote connections among subjects.

Another important consideration in developing objectives is student growth. In other words, how will the unit contribute to higher levels of thinking and personal/social development? Robinson, Ross, and White (1985), have developed the concept of a *growth scheme* which is based on the notion that most educational activities discriminate between less and more complex behaviour. A growth scheme for a particular objective will comprise levels of growth which correspond with less complex to more complex behaviour. To develop a growth scheme, the teacher should attempt to develop a rough scale of development, identify possible dimensions of growth, and describe the possible levels of growth within those dimensions. The chapter on mythology, for example, presents a growth scheme with four developmental levels. The specificity of the growth scheme will be related to the type of objective (instructional, expressive, and Type III), with the instructional objective being the most specific and the expressive being the least specific. However, even the expressive objective will probably contain some conception of more mature performance, although this judgement must come after the student has completed the activity. Readers should consult

Curriculum Development for Effective Instruction (1985) for a much more detailed description of how to develop multidimensional growth schemes.

TEACHING STRATEGIES AND LEARNING EXPERIENCES

Teachers should select instructional strategies that will facilitate the achievement of the identified objectives.

Instructional objectives can be associated with structured, teacher-directed strategies such as recitation, drill, and mastery learning. Mastery learning (Bloom, 1976) involves breaking down curriculum material into small units with which students can work at their own pace. The units also contain specific subcomponents such as concepts and skills. At the end of a unit, the student usually completes a criterion-referenced test to assess whether she or he is ready to move on to the next unit. If the student has not achieved at the appropriate level, then she or he works on the needed skill area. There is evidence that mastery learning produces significant gains in student achievement (Ryan & Schmidt, 1979).

Although teacher-directed strategies have a definite place in integrated studies, we feel that their role is limited. Most strategies such as recitation and drill do not help the student make connections across subjects, let alone within subjects. Mastery learning, with its atomistic thrust of breaking things down into small units, is also better suited to basic skill development than facilitating higher level thinking skills. Thus, mastery learning may precede a unit on integrated studies and have a small role within an integrated program, but it should not be the predominant mode of teaching and learning.

Type III objectives encourage various problem-solving strategies. We have already examined some of these strategies in Chapter 3. Other problem strategies that were not discussed include case studies based on public policy dilemmas, moral dilemmas, and group investigation approaches.

The Canadian Critical Issues series (Bourne & Eisenberg, 1978), contains good examples of the *case-study* approach. This series contains a number of actual historical and current case studies dealing with such issues as the status of women, urbanization, euthanasia, censorship, Native rights, due process, and multiculturalism. In general the approach involves the following steps:

1. Read and discuss a case with sensitivity and open-mindedness toward the various positions taken.

2. Take a stand, if only tentatively, on the issue under consideration.

3. Defend adopted position by giving reasons, invoking principles, and presenting evidence.

4. Argue against opposing views in the same open and rational manner.

5. Modify the position in light of ... dialogue with others. (p. 12)

The issues identified in the series lead naturally to an interdisciplinary approach. In discussing issues such as euthanasia, the case study calls on teachers and students to bring together subjects such as science, psychology, sociology, history, and law. The urbanization issue facilitates inquiry into ecology, urban planning, history, law, sociology, and psychology.

Another approach that can be used in problem solving is the moral *dilemma* approach. Here a problem is presented to the student that contains conflicting values or principles. For example, a teenage girl is in a department store with a friend and the friend decides to shoplift a sweater. After the friend leaves with the sweater, the girl is stopped by security and she is asked to give the name of her friend. This dilemma involves a conflict between loyalty to her friend and telling the truth. Dilemmas are not as disciplined-based as the case studies described above, but they still demand an integrated response from the student. Moral dilemmas are most effective if they are part of a unit and not introduced abstractly out of context.

Often individuals in various religious and spiritual traditions faced dilemmas. For example, Christ was tempted by the devil and Buddha was also tempted while meditating under the Bodhi tree. Arjuna in the *Bhagavad Gita* was faced with the dilemma of whether or not he should fight in the war against people he knew. These dilemmas can be looked at metaphorically and related to our own struggles. Mythological dilemmas deal with universal issues that most humans must confront, thus solving dilemmas based on mythology can move beyond the transactional level to stimulate a transformational response through personal integration in the issue.

A third example of a transactional teaching strategy is the *group investigation* approach developed by Herbert Thelen (1960). This strategy involves small groups of students pursuing a problem through the following stages (adapted from Joyce & Weil, 1986, pp. 237-238):

1. Encounter a puzzling situation (the situation can be planned or unplanned).

2. Explore reactions to the situation.

3. Define the problem and organize procedures to solve the problem (e.g., assign group tasks).

4. Engage in independent and group study.

5.   Analyze progress and process.

6.   Identify a new problem and process.

This procedure might be used in a unit in integrated studies so that small groups of students can work together on a particular topic or problem. The students work co-operatively as the teacher acts as guide and resource. If the students become stuck or engaged in conflict the teacher can intervene to facilitate resolution of the difficulty. Problems that lend themselves to a group investigation approach include pressing social issues (e.g., free trade, role of drugs in sports, environmental problems) and perennial questions that are raised in literature and mythology (struggle for individuality in a conforming society, the challenges and responsibilities of marriage).

Expressive objectives can be best realized through transformational teaching strategies. Several of these strategies (e.g., visualization, role playing, and creative thinking) have already been presented in the previous two chapters. One technique which was not discussed but deserves serious consideration is co-operative learning.

Co-operative learning uses small groups to enhance academic achievement and emotional development. There is ample evidence to support the positive effects of co-operative learning (Slavin, 1983). One popular strategy is the Jigsaw strategy which could also be used in an integrative studies context. In the Jigsaw strategy students are assigned to teams of four or five persons. They read narrative materials such as short stories, biographies, and chapters from texts, and each team member is given a special topic on which to become an expert. The students discuss their topics in "expert groups" and then return to teach their teammates what they have learned. For example, students could each become an "expert" on a particular character in a story. Students would then share their perspectives on their character.

Other methods include student achievement teams (STAD) or the use of teams-games-tournaments (TGT). In the STAD approach students work in pairs or small groups and help each other learn skills or information that is important to the unit. Each small group forms a team within which members help one another so that the overall team performance improves. In TGT method teams compete against one another directly.

Co-operative learning can be used at all three levels — transmission, transaction, and transformation. If it is used solely for improving achievement on low level skill items its focus is transmission. However, much of the rationale for co-operative learning is transformational in nature. For example, in *Together We Learn* (1990), five principles for co-operative learning are proposed and one of these is "students work in positive interdependence." In this approach to learning, students become involved with one another and concerned about the welfare of each person in the group. According to the book, "co-operative learning provides opportunities for all students to develop and to believe in their ability to contribute and learn from others" (p. 11). Clearly this principle is transformational in nature and, if it is used in the context of co-operative learning, the overall approach can be holistic.

EVALUATION STRATEGIES

Referring to Table 4.1, various student evaluation strategies can be linked with orientation, aims, and instructional strategies.

Transmission Evaluation

Evaluation from a transmission orientation focuses on objective tests. Central to objective tests are the concepts of validity and reliability. To be a valid measure, a test must assess what it purports to assess. This is known as face validity. Other forms of validity are concurrent validity and predictive validity. Concurrent validity involves checking to see if other tests of the same concept arrive at similar results. Predictive validity involves assessing whether the test accurately indicates future behaviour (Holmes, 1982, p. 18).

Reliability refers to the idea that a test will give the same results in different circumstances. This means the test can be marked by different trained scorers and the results will be the same. Reliability of tests that assess attitudes is usually not as high as that of tests which assess recall of factual material.

Pratt (1980) concludes that reliability can be increased through three strategies:

1. Increase the number of items on the test.

2. Increase the discrimination of each item. Discrimination refers to the extent to which each item distinguishes between those students who scored highest and those who scored lowest on the test as a whole.

3. Increase the homogeneity of the test. Thus, a test is more reliable if it measures one skill (e.g., spelling) rather than a number of skills (e.g., spelling, punctuation, and vocabulary). (pp. 250-251)

The most common tests include multiple choice, true or false, and completion. These tests could be used in integrative studies to assess students' knowledge of a subject such as mythology. For example, the students could take a short quiz to insure that they understood the basic aspects of the myths that were being studied. Examples of possible items for each of these three types of tests follow:

Multiple Choice:
The designer of the labyrinth where Minotaur lived was:
a) Minos
b) Ariadne
c) Daedalus
d) Theseus

True or False:
The Aegean Sea was named after King Aegeus when he threw himself into the sea because he believed his son, Theseus, had been killed. T or F

Completion:
The slayer of Medusa was _____. (Perseus)

Pratt (1980), provides an excellent discussion of factors that one should consider in developing objective tests.

Transaction Evaluation

Transactional evaluation tends to focus on problem-solving assessment. Ross and Maynes (1982) provide a good discussion of various techniques that can be used to assess problem solving.

Observation is one technique that can be used. Observation schemes can range from the simple to the complex. Simple schemes tend to isolate one skill and focus on observing how students perform in that one area. Complex observation schemes contain several dimensions as well as a growth scheme (see p. 160). In any case, the teacher must be clear about what she or he is looking for and develop some sort of scale or set of observation criteria. For example, if students are working with metaphor, teachers can use the general growth scheme described in terms of four metaphoric levels in Chapter 1 (pp. 10-12). The teacher then observes students to see if they are using metaphor in a simple, symbolic way or if they are using it in an integrative or inventive way.

Observation scales can also be used. Scales focus on whether or not and how often students use the expected criteria. For example, one could make a scale with the different forms of metaphoric thinking, as in Table 4.2, and then check () how often students use the different forms in a group discussion.

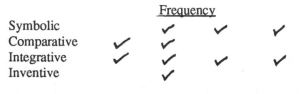

	Frequency		
Symbolic	✓	✓	✓
Comparative	✓	✓		
Integrative	✓	✓	✓	✓
Inventive	✓			

Table 4.2

Ross and Maynes comment that observation tends to be high in validity because it focuses on what students are actually supposed to be doing. However, observation is less reliable because conditions for observation can vary widely and, therefore, produce varying results.

Open-ended tests usually present a problem to which the student makes a written answer. From a transactional perspective the problem presented should provide an opportunity for a full range of responses. Below are two open-ended problems (Ross & Maynes, 1982):

1. Comparative Problem

> Suppose that you had a pen-pal in China. You would probably tell your pen-pal all about the things you like to see and do. Imagine that this pen-pal wanted to know what you do with your spare time at different times of the year.
> Compare what you do with your spare time in the summer to what you do with your spare time in the winter.

2. Decision-Making Problem

> Brucedale, which used to be a small country village, has now become a suburb of [a] city. More shopping is needed for the people who live there. The village council must decide where it should be located. How should they go about making their decision? (p. 157)

Open-ended tests, then, are very appropriate for Type III objectives (see p. 104). Again specific criteria and a general growth scheme can facilitate the marking of the open-ended questions.

Transformation Evaluation

Evaluation from a transformational perspective does not focus on objective knowledge or decision-making skills; instead, there is an emphasis on an assessment of inner development and creativity through interviews, journal writing, marking writing, peer evaluation, and self-evaluation.

Interviews. The interview approach allows the teacher to probe in order to gain a sharper sense of how the student is thinking and feeling. Structured interviews should again reflect the conception of student growth and the criteria associated with the various stages of growth. For example, the teacher could interview students to assess what stage they are working on with their personal mythology. Since personal mythologies can deal with questions of personal meaning, interviews would be an appropriate mechanism for exploring questions related to values and meaning. Some questions and assignments that might be used in a structured interview with students regarding mythology include the following:

1. Choose one of the characters in the myth and describe from that character's point of view the central struggles that she or he faced.

2. What connections can you make between this person's struggles and the struggles of other individuals?

3. What qualities do you see in the hero/ine?

4. Pick one metaphor that you feel is appropriate for the qualities you see.

5. Are there any connections you can make between the hero/ine's story and your own? What are they and what are the reasons for the connections?

One of the main problems with the structured interview is that it is time-consuming and thus difficult to administer. Alternatives to the structured interview are short, informal interviews with students or group interviews where several students are interviewed at once. However, both of these approaches are less reliable and valid than the structured interview with an individual student.

Journal Writing. Journal writing is an important tool for assessing student growth from a transformational perspective. Journals can be kept by both teachers and students. Teachers should keep a journal with their observations of students' behaviour; this provides teachers with an anecdotal record. Journals are less focused than observation scales, but they can allow for the recording of the unique — that is, particular student behaviours that were not anticipated. In short, the journal allows a teacher to record expressive objective outcomes. Teachers may even want to include some samples of student work in their journals, such as drawings and poetry.

Teachers should also use their journals to record their reflections on student work and behaviour. In the journal connections can be made to show how a student is working in different subject areas. For example, a teacher may want to include reflections on how a student's writing and art work are linked. It is best to write in the journal everyday so that the entries are not sporadic. A journal is a critical tool to help teachers become reflective practitioners.

Students can also keep journals, and this practice is often encouraged in writing process programs. Teachers usually have access to student journals, and this expectation is made clear to students. Students should be encouraged to record thoughts and feelings which they are ready to share with teachers and perhaps another student. Journal formats are usually very open; students can include short pieces of prose, poetry, and drawings. Errors in grammar and spelling are not usually marked. Journals could be an important part of the mythology program described in this book as they provide an informal context for developing one's own life story or myth.

Should journals be marked? Teachers differ on this question. It is possible to look at the journals in terms of the students' level of engagement: how deeply have the students engaged themselves in the journals? Do their entries tend to be rather superficial and describe only external events, or do the journals show a recording of the inner life as well as an attempt to reflect on experience?

Marking Writing. Many of the activities suggested in this handbook involve student writing. For example, the chapter on mythology contains a number of written exercises. One possible approach to scoring this work is *holistic scoring.* Holistic scoring is particularly appropriate in integrated studies because it is based on two or more teachers scoring the same pieces of student writing.

Holistic scoring involves teachers giving a student essay a general score (e.g., marking on a scale of 1 to 10) based on an overall impression of the writing. Another teacher makes a similar impression score and the average of the two scores provides the basis for the mark. It is even better if more than two teachers can score the essays. There are different approaches to holistic scoring. In one approach, there is no attempt to agree on standards and criteria as teachers simply score the writing based on an overall impression. Another approach is for the teachers to agree before the marking what each score means so that a 9 or 10 denotes that the essay involves a high degree of creativity as well as being well written. This latter approach is more reliable, of course, but requires more time, and the holistic approach of scoring based on an overall impression can break down (Holmes, 1982, p. 74).

If it is not possible to involve other teachers, then the teacher should develop a scoring scheme based on criteria. From an integrated studies/holistic perspective, this scheme should encourage creativity and making connections. A sample scheme might include the following criteria:

1. Originality of thought   20

2. Expression, Imagery   20

3. Connectiveness   20
   (e.g., degree to which the essay makes connections between ideas and subjects, or provokes connections through metaphor)

4. Clarity and Organization   20

5. Grammar and Spelling   20

Of course, the criteria can vary with the context and purpose of the essay. Holmes (1982) argues that holistic scoring is appropriate for a summative mark, but does not provide the student with any constructive feedback. However, a scoring system based on criteria, such as the ones identified above, can be linked to instruction: teachers can focus on the identified criteria to facilitate student growth in those areas.

Peer Evaluation. Students can help each other with their writing. The teacher may want to use learning partners or a "buddy" system where two students work with each other. By working with one other student, trust can be developed so that an appropriate atmosphere is developed for feedback. It is helpful if students have a checklist based on the key evaluation criteria of the lesson to help guide their editing process. Since good writing is basically editing and rewriting, peer editing can help support this overall process.

Self-Evaluation. Students should use the criteria checklist mentioned above to assess their own work. After self-editing, they can involve their partner and then the teacher in the final editing process. Self-evaluation can be done not only in writing, but in other areas (social skills, thinking skills, etc.) involved in an integrated studies program. Teachers may want to develop a self-report questionnaire based on unit objectives so that students can assess their own performance.

SUMMARY

In developing units in integrated studies we encourage teachers to work in a manner consistent with their curriculum orientation. For example, it does not make much sense to evaluate problem-solving skills with a true or false test that simply focuses on information recall. In general, we should try to develop programs which are congruent with respect to orientation, objectives, strategies, and evaluation procedures. Recalling the nested relationship of the orientations shown in the first chapter, we note here that the transformation position, or a holistic approach, allows the teacher the most flexibility since it incorporates the widest range of strategies. At the same time it is the most challenging position for the teacher since the various strategies cannot be randomly selected, but instead should be linked in an integrative manner. As we have noted already in the summary of Chapter 1, this integration can occur through a reflective approach to teaching which encourages the teacher to trust her or his intuition.

REFERENCES

Bloom, B. S. (1976). *Human characteristics and school learning.* New York: McGraw-Hill.

Bourne, P., & Eisenberg, J. (1978). *Social issues in the curriculum: Theory, practice and evaluation.* Toronto: OISE Press.

Clarke, J., Widerman, B., & Eadie, S. (1990). *Together we learn*. Toronto: Prentice-Hall.

Eisner, E. (1985). *The art of educational evaluation: A personal view*. Philadelphia: Falmer Press.

Holmes, M. (1982). *What every teacher and parent should know about student evaluation*. Toronto: OISE Press.

Joyce, B., & Weil, M. (1986) *Models of Teaching*. Englewood Cliffs, NJ: Prentice-Hall.

Pratt, D. (1980). *Curriculum, design and development*. New York: Harcourt, Brace, Jovanovich.

Ryan, D., & Schmidt, M. (1979). *Mastery learning: Theory, research and implementation*. Toronto: Ministry of Education.

Robinson, F., Ross, J., & White, F. (1985). *Curriculum development for effective instruction*. Toronto: OISE Press.

Ross, J. A., & Maynes, F. J. (1982). *Teaching problem-solving*. Toronto: OISE Press.

Slavin, R. E. (1983). *Cooperative learning*. New York: Longman.

Thelen, H. A. (1960). *Education and the human quest*. New York: Harper & Row.

CHAPTER 5

IMPLEMENTING INTEGRATED STUDIES

The past two decades have produced significant research in the area of curriculum implementation (Fullan, 1982; Leithwood, 1982; Hall & Loucks, 1978). One lesson learned from this research is that we cannot simply develop programs and then expect them to be used by teachers without providing planning and support. This research has helped us recognize that implementation is not one particular event, but instead is a complex process occurring over a long period of time. It is also possible to view implementation from the three curriculum positions (see Table 5.1).

From a transmission position implementation is viewed narrowly and teachers are expected to implement the program exactly as the developers intended. Often "teacher-proof" curricula are developed and disseminated with very little accompanying in-service or professional development offered to the classroom teachers. From a transaction perspective, implementation is viewed as a process that allows a teacher to adapt the curriculum according to the needs of her or his classroom. Teachers are encouraged to reflect on the new program as they use it. Finally, a transformation position encourages teachers to engage the implementation process holistically. Teachers are encouraged to not only reflect on the program cognitively, but also to react to the program in terms of its emotional impact. Most importantly, from a transformation perspective, implementation is viewed as an inside-out process (Hunt, 1987) that begins with the inner life of the teacher. The inside-out process is based on the view that a teacher's common sense ideas and unexpressed theories, which have grown out of practical experience, are enormously important and must be considered in any change process. Too often implementation has been a top down, outside-in process devoid of meaning to both teachers and students.

One of the most comprehensive studies on implementation, the RAND Corporation study (Berman & McLaughlin, 1978), supports the effectiveness of transactional and transformational approaches. It was found that transmission implementation strategies such as packaged management approaches, one-shot workshops, formal evaluation, and the use of outside consultants rendered poor results. On the other hand, teacher involvement in decision making, local development of materials, observation of similar projects in other classrooms, regular meetings that focus on solving specific problems, and direct classroom assistance led to effective use of new programs.

	TRANSMISSION	TRANSACTION	TRANSFORMATION
Study of New Programs	Focus on Content	Focus on how teaching methodologies affect processes	Focus on how program affects the whole child
Resources	Textbooks	Variety of resources to stimulate mental processes	Human resources are stressed as personal growth of teachers is central
Roles	Roles fixed within system hierarchy	Roles more flexible, which allows for inter-action among teachers	Roles very flexible with emphasis on I-thou relationship among teachers
Professional Development (P.D.)	General P.D. sessions that focus on information trans-mission	More individualized P.D. with stress on practice, feedback and coaching	Individualized P.D. with emphasis on coaching and personal growth for teachers
Timeline	Short timeline, implementation seen as event not process	Reasonable, flexible timeline as implement-ation seen as process not event	Long, flexible timeline as implementation is seen as holistic process
Communication System	One-way, top-down communication	Two-way, interactive communication	Two-way interactive communication that goes beyond cognitive elements
Monitoring System	Focus on accountability with use of tests	Varitey of methods used to monitor progress	Informal methods are used, particularly teacher feedback

Table 5.1

Note. From *Curriculum: Perspectives and Practice*, (p. 294) by J. Miller and W. Seller, (in press), Mississauga, ON: Copp Clark Pitman. Copyright 1990 by Copp Clark Pitman. Reprinted by permission.

Clearly the use of integrated studies also demands a transactional or transformational approach to implementation. Integration can occur through one teacher attempting to integrate subjects within a single classroom setting, or through two or more teachers collaborating to teach an integrated unit. In either case implementation needs to be approached reflectively and from the inside-out.

What then are some strategies that should be considered in implementing integrated studies? In this chapter approaches that teachers may find helpful are discussed from both a group and individual perspective. First, staff development initiatives are discussed. Ideally, more than one teacher will be involved in using integrated studies and certain staff development strategies would facilitate the process. Second, one staff development approach, coaching, is discussed in some detail since it allows two teachers to work together on using a new program. Finally, the several strategies that individual teachers can employ are discussed; these strategies include the use of teacher narrative (Connelly & Clandinin, 1988), metaphor, and the C-RE-A-T-E cycle (Hunt, 1987).

STAFF DEVELOPMENT

Staff development involves adult learning and growth. Brundage and Mackerarcher (1980) have made an extensive analysis of basic principles of adult learning. Some of the key principles include:

1. Adult learning is facilitated when past experience is applied to current learning through divergent thinking processes. "These include metaphors, analogies, graphs, figures, drawings, games and so on." (p. 99)

2. Adult learning is facilitated by a psychologically safe learning environment where the individual feels comfortable in trying our new behaviours.

3. Adult learning is facilitated when it is related directly to the individual's current needs and problems.

4. Adult learning will be most satisfying when it is self-directed.

5. Adult learning is facilitated when expectations are clear and precise and feedback is immediate.

6. Adult learning is facilitated by two-way communication between the teacher and learner which encourages learner reflection.

7. Adult learning is facilitated when the individual does not feel pressured by arbitrary time limits.

8.   Adult learning is facilitated when the teacher/facilitator recognizes and accommodates different learning styles.

9.   Adult learning is facilitated when the teacher relinquishes some control over the instructional process and shares this process with the learner.

10. Adult learning is facilitated when there is a variety of individual and group learning activities.

The RAND study cited earlier identified factors associated with successful efforts in the area of staff development. These factors are congruent with the principles just cited. One of the factors is recognizing the expertise of the teacher with regard to the practice of teaching. In other words, the teacher is viewed as a valuable resource person who helps share in the direction of the staff development program (principle 4).

A second factor is local adaptation. Any attempt at curriculum change should involve, to a certain extent, "reinventing the wheel," whereby the principal and staff make sense of the new program in their own terms. Thus, if a school staff is attempting an integrated studies program they must work out their own approach. They may use units and materials already developed, but they must work through the materials so that they see how they can relate the materials to their own programs (principle 3).

A third factor is that professional growth is long-term and non-linear. Implementation often takes several years to occur (principle 7).

A fourth factor which facilitates change is the reduction of the psychological risks of change. This occurs when administrators become involved in the process (principles 2 and 9).

A fifth factor in successful staff development is that staff development is not a special program, but an ongoing part of the organizational life of a school.

Joyce, Hersh, and McKibbon (1983, pp. 139-142) identify five components of a staff development program. These include:

1.   Presentation of theory
2.   Modeling or demonstration
3.   Practice under simulated conditions
4.   Structured feedback
5.   Coaching for application

Again a number of the principles of adult learning apply to these components, particularly the last three which are critical to a staff development program. The first two components focus on the theory of the approach and demonstrate how the new program (e.g., problem solving) can be used. The final three components allow the teacher to try out the new approach. The third component asks the teacher to try the approach in a safe situation where mistakes will not affect student performance. This component might be pursued in a workshop setting with colleagues whom the teacher knows and trusts (principle 2). After the teacher has tried out the approach, colleagues can offer constructive feedback to the teacher (principle 5).

The most important part of the process is coaching. One teacher (coach) works with another teacher (partner) in the classroom setting to facilitate the partner's work with the new program. Coaching has been found to be a successful tool for professional growth because again it rests on many of the key principles of adult learning. For example, coaching is based on two-way communication that encourages teacher reflection on practice (principle 6). It is also focused and specific, and allows for direct feedback (principle 5). Coaching tends to be self-directed (principle 4) since the agenda and objectives are set by the teacher. Coaching is also a long-term process that does not involve arbitrary time restrictions (principle 7).

Teachers developing and implementing units in integrated studies find that coaching facilitates their use of the new programs in their classrooms. Seller (in press) suggests the following coaching strategy:

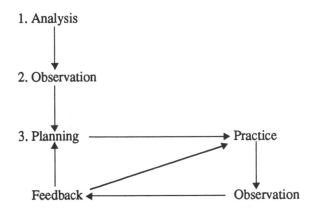

Figure 5.1

1. *Analysis.* In this first step, the coach attempts to gain an understanding of the relationship of the new program, in this case a unit in integrated studies, to the practice of her or his partner. The partner explains to the coach what she or he is trying to do with the new unit and how it relates to the overall program in her or

his classroom. The coach clarifies for herself or himself the objectives, teaching strategies, and resources that the partner will be using.

2. *Observation.* The coach visits and observes the partner's classroom. This first visit allows the coach to become familiar with the partner's classroom, and provides a baseline for further observations and discussions with the partner. During this initial day of observation the coach does not address the use of the integrated studies, but merely attempts to confirm the image of the classroom developed during the analysis (step 1).

3. *Planning.* The partner and the coach develop an image of what the classroom will look like as a result of implementing the new unit. This image may focus on teaching strategies, student learning, and the resources involved. The coach should help ensure that the image is attainable.

   The coach and partner should also help identify the steps that will be needed to achieve the desired image. Again, the steps should be realistic and appropriate. The coach can assist the partner in solving any problems that the partner may encounter in the process.

   Finally, the partner and coach should agree on an observation schedule and the criteria for determining whether the unit in integrated studies is being successfully used.

4. *Using the Plan.* The partner begins to try out the new unit. She or he may find it helpful to visit the classroom of the coach or another classroom where integrated studies is being used.

   After the partner has had an opportunity to begin the new unit, the coach observes how the unit is being implemented. The coach can keep notes to share with the partner during the feedback session, at which time the coach shares her or his perceptions in relation to the criteria developed during the planning stage. The partner, of course, has an opportunity to share her or his perceptions of the class and her or his reactions to the coach's perceptions. The coach and partner then discuss the next step that the partner will work on and set a date for the next meeting. This process is repeated until both the coach and the partner feel the new unit has been successfully implemented.

   Coaching is an important aspect of any staff development work because it provides a vehicle where teachers can work together in a non-threatening manner. There is ample research to indicate that teaching tends to be a lonely profession in which teachers rarely collaborate with one another (Fullan, 1982; Lortie, 1975; Sarason, 1982). In contrast, coaching provides psychological support, professional companionship, and technical assistance.

Teacher as Reflective Practitioner

Underlying the coaching process and most transactional or transformational approaches to staff development and professional growth is the concept of the reflective practitioner (Schön, 1983). The reflective practitioner moves beyond a technical approach to her or his work, to examining that work from a number of perspectives. The reflective practitioner sees herself or himself as someone who can facilitate learning and problem solving, rather than as an expert with knowledge to transfer to students. She or he is also open to both her or his feelings and the feelings of students (Schön, p. 300).

Metaphor and Narrative

It is also possible to approach staff development and coaching holistically. Two vehicles that can facilitate holistic learning are metaphor and narrative. Hunt (1987) has found that teachers can develop metaphors to clarify their own view of how they teach. A few of the metaphors developed by teachers in Hunt's graduate class include:

+ My class is like a family.

+ I'm a conductor on a train (the learning) and passengers (clients) get on and off when they decide. They choose their own destinations.

+ My work is like an open door/fruitful tree.

+ My work is like... a free-flowing handful of sand. (pp. 77-78)

Another student identified her metaphor as a gurgling, rushing stream:

When I first reflected upon this metaphor as it came during the guided imagery, the essential descriptors were: life-giving, active, pervasive, peaceful, harmonious, not fearful. Some of the important statements were:

+ passing this way but once, make the best possible use of this time and these opportunities;

+ want to leave others happy, invigorated, knowing their own worth and aware of their own inner and outer resources;

+ influencing and being influenced (the two-way opening and sharing process).

Later reflection revealed the apparent contradiction of adjectives, i.e., gurgling and gushing.... My metaphor seems to be depicting the diversity within myself to adapt itself to those students who need (gurgling) a more even, enthusiastic, co-responsible, cheerful and supportive environment. This is definitely more in keeping with my usual human interactions and teaching approach. However, I am capable of strength (gushing), seeming strictness, and maintaining control.... Perhaps with time, more experience, increased confidence, and quiet reflection I will be able to integrate these two life forces into one. The metaphor conveys that vision, that hope. (pp. 79-80)

Metaphor can be very helpful during the analysis stage of coaching as it encourages teachers to take a transformational or holistic approach to identifying the image they have of their own teaching. It might also be helpful for identifying the desired image of implementing integrated studies. For example, the desired effect of integrated learning could be defined in terms of a confluence of streams. Some teachers may not feel comfortable using metaphors, but Hunt suggests that metaphor has become an extremely useful tool in inside-out approaches to change.

Connelly and Clandinin (1988) also have found in their work that metaphor is an important tool which stimulates teachers to reflect on their own practice. Metaphor can become part of what Connelly and Clandinin identify as a teacher's personal narrative. Narrative allows us to think about our life and work as a whole; it is "a kind of life story, larger and more sweeping than the short stories that compose it" (p. 24). Through narrative we try to get at the texture of a teacher's life and how that texture is manifested in teaching. Below is an excerpt from one teacher's journal that includes reflections on another teacher's (Rosita's) work:

When you think about your past, it is important to think about your own experiences as a text. Also, try to think about what has been observed in the classroom as a text. Look at what the teacher does — what the children do....

Rosita's story was like reading a story in a history text. She made history come alive. I can't help but think that she must have had to have a lot of strength and courage. You could read it in her face. It had to be so difficult to be working for the board on the one hand and vice-chairman of the Renegade Board on the other. Now I'm beginning to see what is meant by: "Think of your own experience as a text." (Connelly & Clandinin, 1988, p. 213)

The use of narrative allows a teacher to see the important themes in her or his life in relation to the practice of teaching. Images and metaphors help frame the themes that emerge so that the meaning and direction of one's life and work become clearer.

It may be helpful in staff development and coaching to have the coach and partner explore the partner's personal narrative and how integrated studies can relate to this narrative. Again, this approach will depend on the orientation of the teacher; transmission-oriented teachers may not be drawn to the use of personal narrative.

C-RE-A-T-E Cycle

David Hunt (1987) has developed a variation on Kolb's (1984) learning cycle which allows teachers to reflect on their own practice. The five steps in Hunt's C-RE-A-T-E cycle are:

1. *Concern:* State your concern (e.g., I am concerned about using integrated studies in my classroom).

2. *Reflect:* Summarize your implicit theories or beliefs (e.g., your orientation) through the use of metaphor or narrative.

3. *Analyze:* Apply your beliefs and practitioner knowledge through the development of an action plan.

4. *Try Out:* Use the action plan.

5. *Experience:* Examine feedback from the action, re-evaluate the action, and go through the cycle again. (adapted from p. 157)

Hunt describes using the cycle in an example of a school counselor working with a 15-year-old student who was about to be expelled from school for her aggressive behaviour (concern). The reflection stage revealed that the counselor needed a new metaphor to frame this problem. The new metaphor which emerged involved a magician trying to balance plates on the top of long rods while moving back and forth. This metaphor highlighted the need for the counselor to act quickly before the student was expelled. In the next stage (analysis) the counselor realized that the student was a "doer" who learned through active experimentation so that any strategies applied would have to be action-oriented. The counselor recommended the student become involved in a co-op program where she would help out in an after school drop-in program. The strategy worked and the student's behaviour became less aggressive. Along with coaching, metaphor, and personal narrative, the C-RE-A-T-E cycle can become a vehicle for developing whole teachers and holistic learning.

CONCLUSION

At the center of an integrated program and a holistic approach is a teacher. Although we have presented a number of strategies and techniques in this book, it should be understood that subject integration is linked to teacher integration. If a teacher is feeling alienated and fragmented, then it is not reasonable to expect her or him to develop and effectively teach integrated studies. In *The Holistic Curriculum*, Miller (1988) has discussed the need for authenticity and caring in teachers. Teachers should be genuine in their approach and not be playing some false role which can alienate students. Secondly, they should be caring (Noddings, 1984) and compassionate (Miller, 1981). Caring and compassion involve some sensitivity to the inner life of the student; without this sensitivity the holistic curriculum and integrated studies become empty. The senior author (Miller, 1981) has long advocated various centering and meditative methods for teachers so that they can awaken more fully to their inner life. By awakening to our inner life, we can simultaneously connect to the inner life of our students. This connection is fundamental to the holistic curriculum and to integrated learning.

REFERENCES

Berman, P., & McLaughlin, M. W. (1978). *Federal programs supporting educational change: Vol. IV. Summary*. Santa Monica, CA: RAND Corporation.

Brundage, D. H., & Mackeracher, D. (1980). *Adult learning principles and their application to program planning*. Toronto: Ministry of Education.

Connelly, E. M., & Clandinin, D. J. (1988). *Teachers as curriculum planners: Narratives of experience*. Toronto: OISE Press.

Fullan, M. (1982). *The meaning of educational change*. Toronto: OISE Press.

Hall, G. E., & Loucks, S. (1978). Teacher concerns as a basis for facilitating and personalizing staff development. *Teachers College Record, 80*(1), 36-53.

Hunt, D. (1987). *Beginning with ourselves: In practice, theory, and human affairs*. Toronto: OISE Press.

Joyce, B. R., Hersh, R. H., & McKibbon, M. (1983). *The structure of school improvement*. New York: Longman.

Kolb, D. A. (1984). *Experiential learning: Experience as the source of learning and development*. Englewood Cliffs, NJ: Prentice-Hall.

Leithwood, K. A. (1982). *Studies in curriculum decision making*. Toronto: OISE Press.

Lortie, D. C. (1975). *Schoolteacher: A sociological study.* Chicago: University of Chicago Press.

Miller, J. P. (1981). *The compassionate teacher: How to teach and learn with your whole self.* Englewood Cliffs, NJ: Prentice-Hall.

Miller, J. P. (1988). *The holistic curriculum.* Toronto: OISE Press.

Miller, J. P. & Seller, W. (1990). *Curriculum: Perspectives and practice.* Toronto: Copp Clark Pitman.

Noddings, N. (1984). *Caring: Feminine approach to ethics and moral education.* Berkeley, CA: University of California Press.

Sarason, S. B. (1982). *The culture of the school and the problem of change* (2nd. ed.). Boston: Allyn and Bacon.

Seller, W. (in press). A coaching model for utilizing in-school resources. *Capstone Journal of Education.*

Schön, D. (1983). *The reflective practitioner.* New York: Basic Books.

Zee, A. (1986). *Fearful symmetry: The search for beauty in modern physics.* New York: MacMillan.

Appendix A

OISE FIELD CENTRE LOCATIONS

Centre for Principal Development
OISE
252 Bloor Street West
Room 7-234
Toronto, Ontario M5S 1V6

Midnorthern Centre
Centre du Moyen-Nord
École Publique Jeanne Sauvé
296 Van Horne Street
Sudbury, Ontario P3B 1H9

Midwestern Centre
Margaret Avenue Senior School
325 Louisa Street
Kitchener, Ontario N2H 5N1

Niagara Centre
Connaught Public School
28 Prince Street
St. Catharines, Ontario L2R 3X7

Northeastern Centre
King George Public School
550 Harvey Street
North Bay, Ontario P1B 4H3

Northwestern Centre
Heath Park School
1115 Yonge Street
Thunder Bay, Ontario P7E 2T6

Ottawa Valley Centre
60 Tiverton Drive
Nepean, Ontario K2E 6L8

Trent Valley Centre
Box 719
150 O'Carroll Avenue
Peterborough, Ontario K9J 7A1

OISE/UWO Educational Leadership
Centre
1137 Western Road
London, Ontario N6G 1G7